MTEL 01 Communication and Literacy Skills
Teacher Certification Exam

By: Sharon Wynne, M.S.
Southern Connecticut State University

"And, while there's no reason yet to panic, I think it's only prudent that we make preparations to panic."

XAMonline, INC.
Boston

To obtain permission(s) to use the material from this work for any purpose including workshops or seminars, please submit a written request to

XAMonline, Inc.
21 Orient Ave.
Melrose, MA 02176
Toll Free 1-800-509-4128
Email: info@xamonline.com
Web: www.xamonline.com
Fax: 1-781-662-9268

Library of Congress Cataloging-in-Publication Data
Wynne, Sharon A.
MTEL: Communication and Literacy Skills   01 Teacher Certification / Sharon A. Wynne.
   ISBN: 978-1-58197-287-0
1. MTEL: Communication and Literacy Skills 01 2. Study Guides. 3. MTEL
4. Teachers' Certification & Licensure. 5. Careers

Managing Editor	Dr. Harte Weiner, Ph. D.
Copy Editor	Susan Andres, M.A.
Assistant Editor	Anna Wong, B.S.
Production Coordinator	David Aronson

Disclaimer:
The opinions expressed in this publication are the sole works of XAMonline and were created independently from the National Education Association (NES), Educational Testing Service (ETS), or any State Department of Education, National Evaluation Systems or other testing affiliates. Between the time of publication and printing, state specific standards as well as testing formats and website information may change that are not included in part or in whole within this product. XAMonline develops sample test questions, and they reflect similar content as on real tests; however, they are not former tests. XAMonline assembles content that aligns with state standards but makes no claims nor guarantees teacher candidates a passing score. Numerical scores are determined by testing companies such as NES or ETS and then are compared with individual state standards. A passing score varies from state to state.

Printed in the United States of America   œ-1
MTEL: Communication and Literacy Skills 01
ISBN: 978-1-58197-287-0

Table of Contents

Great Study and Testing Tips!

What to study in order to prepare for the subject assessments is the focus of this study guide but equally important is *how* you study.

You can increase your chances of truly mastering the information by taking some simple but effective steps.

Study Tips:

1. <u>Some foods aid the learning process</u>. Foods such as milk, nuts, seeds, rice, and oats help your study efforts by releasing natural memory enhancers called CCKs (*cholecystokinin*) composed of *tryptophan*, *choline*, and *phenylalanine*. All of these chemicals enhance the neurotransmitters associated with memory. Before studying, try a light, protein-rich meal of eggs, turkey, and fish. All of these foods release the memory enhancing chemicals. The better the connections, the more you comprehend.

Likewise, before you take a test, stick to a light snack of energy-boosting and relaxing foods. A glass of milk, a piece of fruit, or some peanuts all release various memory-boosting chemicals and help you to relax and focus on the subject at hand.

2. <u>Learn to take great notes</u>. A by-product of our modern culture is that we have grown accustomed to getting our information in short doses (i.e. TV news sound bites or *USA Today*-style newspaper articles.)

Consequently, we have subconsciously trained ourselves to assimilate information better in <u>neat little packages</u>. If your notes are scrawled all over the paper, it fragments the flow of the information. Strive for clarity. Newspapers use a standard format to achieve clarity. Your notes can be much clearer with proper formatting. A very effective format is called the <u>*Cornell Method.*</u>

> Take a sheet of loose-leaf lined notebook paper and draw a line all the way down the paper about 1"–2" from the left-hand edge.

> Draw another line across the width of the paper about 1"–2" up from the bottom. Repeat this process on the reverse side of the page.

Look at the highly effective result. You have ample room for notes, a left-hand margin for special emphasis items or inserting supplementary data from the textbook, a large area at the bottom for a brief summary, and a little rectangular space for just about anything you want.

3. <u>Get the concept then the details</u>. Too often, we focus on the details and do not gather an understanding of the concept. However, if you simply memorize only dates, places, or names, you may well miss the whole point of the subject.

A key way to understand things is to put them in your own words. If you are working from a textbook, automatically summarize each paragraph in your mind. If you are outlining text, do not simply copy the author's words.

Rephrase them in your own words. You remember your own thoughts and words much better than someone else's and subconsciously tend to associate the important details with the core concepts.

4. <u>Ask why?</u> Pull apart written material paragraph by paragraph and do not forget the captions under the illustrations.

Example: If the heading is "Stream Erosion," flip it around to read, "Why do streams erode?" Then answer the questions.

If you train your mind to think in a series of questions and answers, not only will you learn more, but it also helps to lessen the test anxiety because you are used to answering questions.

5. <u>Read for reinforcement and future needs</u>. Even if you only have ten minutes, put your notes or a book in your hand. Your mind is similar to a computer; you have to input data in order to have it processed. *By reading, you are creating the neural connections for future retrieval.* The more times you read something, the more you reinforce the learning of ideas.

Even if you do not fully understand something on the first pass, *your mind stores much of the material for later recall.*

6. <u>Relax to learn, so go into exile.</u> Our bodies respond to an inner clock called biorhythms. Burning the midnight oil works well for some people, but not everyone.

If possible, set aside a particular place to study that is free of distractions. Shut off the television, cell phone, and pager and exile your friends and family during your study period.

If you really are bothered by silence, try background music. Light classical music at a low volume has been shown to aid in concentration over other types. Music without lyrics that evokes pleasant emotions is highly suggested. Try just about anything by Mozart. It relaxes you.

7. <u>Use arrows not highlighters.</u> At best, it is difficult to read a page full of yellow, pink, blue, and green streaks. Try staring at a neon sign for a while and you will soon see that the horde of colors obscures the message.

A quick note, a brief dash of color, an underline, and an arrow pointing to a particular passage is much clearer than a horde of highlighted words.

8. <u>**Budget your study time.**</u> Although you should not ignore any of the material, *allocate your available study time in the same ratio that topics may appear on the test.*

Testing Tips:

1. <u>Get smart; play dumb</u>. Do not read anything into the question. Do not assume that the test writer is looking for something else than what is asked. Stick to the question as written and do not read extra things into it.

2. <u>Read the question and all the choices *twice* before answering the question</u>. You may miss something by not carefully reading and then re-reading both the question and the answers.

If you really do not have a clue as to the right answer, leave it blank the first time through. Go on to the other questions, as they may provide a clue as to how to answer the skipped questions.

If later on, you still cannot answer the skipped ones . . . ***guess.*** The only penalty for guessing is that you *might* get it wrong. Only one thing is certain; if you do not put anything down, you will get it wrong!

3. <u>Turn the question into a statement</u>. Look at the way the questions are worded. The syntax of the question usually provides a clue. Does it seem more familiar as a statement rather than as a question? Does it sound strange?

By turning a question into a statement, you may be able to spot if an answer sounds right, and it may trigger memories of material you have read.

4. <u>Look for hidden clues</u>. It is actually very difficult to compose multiple-foil (choice) questions without giving away part of the answer in the options presented.

In most multiple-choice questions, you can often readily eliminate one or two of the potential answers. This leaves you with only two real possibilities and automatically your odds go to fifty-fifty with very little work.

5. <u>Trust your instincts</u>. For every fact that you read, you subconsciously retain something of that knowledge. On questions about which you are not really certain, go with your basic instincts. **Your first impression on how to answer a question is usually correct.**

6. <u>Mark your answers directly on the test booklet</u>. Do not bother trying to fill in the optical scan sheet on the first pass through the test.

Be careful not to mismark your answers when you transcribe them to the scan sheet.

7. <u>Watch the clock</u>! You have a set amount of time to answer the questions. Do not get bogged down trying to answer a single question at the expense of ten questions you can more readily answer.

COMPETENCY 1.0 DETERMINING THE MEANING OF WORDS AND PHRASES

Skill 1.1 Using context clues to determine the meaning of a word with multiple meanings

Context clues help readers determine the meanings of unfamiliar words. The context of a word is the sentence or sentences that surround the word.

Read the following sentences, and attempt to determine the meanings of the words in bold print.

> The **luminosity** of the room was so incredible that there was no need for lights.

If there were no need for lights, then one must assume that the word luminosity has something to do with giving off light. The definition of luminosity is *the emission of light.*

> Jamie could not understand Joe's feelings. His mood swings made understanding him somewhat of an **enigma.**

The fact that he could not be understood made him somewhat of a puzzle. The definition of enigma is *a mystery or puzzle.*

Familiarity with word **roots** (the basic elements of words) and with **prefixes** can help one determine the meanings of unknown words. Following is a partial list of roots and prefixes. It might be useful to review these.

Root	Meaning	Example
aqua	water	aqualung
astro	stars	astrology
bio	life	biology
carn	meat	carnivorous
circum	around	circumnavigate
geo	earth	geology
herb	plant	herbivorous
mal	bad	malicious
neo	new	neonatal
tele	distant	telescope

Prefix	Meaning	Example
un-	not	unnamed
re-	again	reenter
il-	not	illegible
pre-	before	preset
mis-	incorrectly	misstate
in-	not	informal
anti-	against	antiwar
de-	opposite	derail
post-	after	postwar
ir-	not	irresponsible

Word forms

Sometimes a very familiar word can appear as a different part of speech. For example, you may have heard that *fraud* involves a criminal misrepresentation, so when it appears as the adjective form *fraudulent*, (e.g., "He was suspected of *fraudulent* activities.") you can make an educated guess. You probably know that something out-of-date is *obsolete;* therefore, when you read about "built-in *obsolescence,*" you can detect the meaning of the unfamiliar word.

Practice Questions: Read the following sentences and attempt to determine the meanings of the underlined words.

1. Farmer John got a two-horse plow and went to work. Straight <u>furrows</u> stretched out behind him.

    The word <u>furrows</u> means

    - (A) long cuts made by a plow
    - (B) vast, open fields
    - (C) rows of corn
    - (D) pairs of hitched horses

2. The survivors struggled ahead, <u>shambling</u> through the terrible cold, doing their best not to fall.

    The word <u>shambling</u> means

    - (A) frozen in place
    - (B) running
    - (C) shivering uncontrollably
    - (D) walking awkwardly

Answers:

1. (A) is the correct answer. The word *straight* and the expression *stretched out behind him* are your clues.

2. (D) is the correct answer. The words *ahead* and *through* are your clues.

The context for a word is the written passage that surrounds it. Sometimes the writer offers synonyms—words that have nearly the same meaning. Context clues can appear within the sentence itself, within the preceding and/or following sentence(s), or in the passage as a whole.

Sentence clues

Often, a writer will actually **define** a difficult or particularly important word for you the first time it appears in a passage. Phrases such as *that is, such as, which is,* or *is called* might announce the writer's intention to give just the definition you need. Occasionally, a writer will simply use a synonym (a word that means the same thing) or a near-synonym joined by the word *or.* Look at the following examples:

> The <u>credibility</u>, that is to say the believability, of the witness was called into question by evidence of previous perjury.

> Nothing would <u>assuage</u> or lessen the child's grief.

Punctuation at the sentence level is often a clue to the meaning of a word. Commas, parentheses, quotation marks, and dashes tell the reader that the writer is offering a definition.

> A tendency toward <u>hyperbole</u>, extravagant exaggeration, is a common flaw among persuasive writers.

> Political <u>apathy</u>—lack of interest—can lead to the death of the state.

A writer might simply give an **explanation** in other words that you can understand in the same sentence.

> The <u>xenophobic</u> townspeople were suspicious of every foreigner.

Writers also explain a word in terms of its **opposite** at the sentence level.

> His <u>incarceration</u> was ended, and he was elated to be out of jail.

Skill 1.2   Using the context of a paragraph or passage as a clue to the meaning of an unfamiliar or uncommon word or phrase

Adjacent sentence clues

The context for a word goes beyond the sentence in which it appears. At times, the writer uses adjacent (adjoining) sentences to present an explanation or definition.

> *The two dollars for the car repair would have to come out of the <u>contingency</u> fund. Fortunately, Angela's father had taught her to keep some money set aside for just such emergencies.*

Analysis: The second sentence offers a clue to the definition of *contingency* as used in this sentence—*emergencies*. Therefore, a fund for contingencies would be money tucked away for unforeseen and/or urgent events.

Entire passage clues

On occasion, you must look at an entire paragraph or passage to figure out the definition of a word or term. In the following paragraph, notice how the word *nostalgia* undergoes a form of extended definition throughout the selection rather than in just one sentence.

> *The word <u>nostalgia</u> links Greek words for "away from home" and "pain." If you are feeling <u>nostalgic</u>, then you are probably in some physical distress or discomfort, suffering from a feeling of alienation and separation from loved ones or loved places. <u>Nostalgia</u> is that awful feeling you remember the first time you went away to camp or spent the weekend with a friend's family—homesickness, or some condition even more painful than that. However, in common use, <u>nostalgia</u> has come to have associations that are more sentimental. A few years back, for example, a <u>nostalgia</u> craze had to do with the 1950s. We resurrected poodle skirts and saddle shoes, built new restaurants to look like old ones, and tried to make chicken à la king just as mother probably never made it. In TV situation comedies, we recreated a pleasant world that probably never existed and relished our <u>nostalgia</u>, longing for a homey, comfortable lost time.*

Skill 1.3   Determining the meaning of a figurative expression from its context in a paragraph or passage

1. **Simile**: Direct comparison between two things. For example, "My love is like a red-red rose."
2. **Metaphor**: Indirect comparison between two things; the use of a word or phrase denoting one kind of object or action in place of another to suggest a comparison between them. While poets use them extensively, they are also integral to everyday speech. For example, chairs are said to have "legs" and "arms," although we know that it is humans and other animals that have these appendages.
3. **Parallelism**: The arrangement of ideas in phrases, sentences, and paragraphs that balance one element with another of equal importance and similar wording. An example from Francis Bacon's *Of Studies:* "Reading maketh a full man, conference a ready man, and writing an exact man."
4. **Personification**: Human characteristics are attributed to an inanimate object, an abstract quality, or animal. Examples: John Bunyan wrote characters named Death, Knowledge, Giant Despair, Sloth, and Piety in his *Pilgrim's Progress.* The metaphor of an arm of a chair is a form of personification.
5. **Euphemism**: The substitution of an agreeable or inoffensive term for one that might offend or suggest something unpleasant. Many euphemisms, such as *passed away, crossed over,* or nowadays, *passed,* are used to refer to death to avoid using the real word.
6. **Hyperbole**: Deliberate exaggeration for effect or comic effect. An example from Shakespeare's *The Merchant of Venice*:
   > Why, if two gods should play some heavenly match
   > And on the wager lay two earthly women,
   > And Portia one, there must be something else
   > Pawned with the other, for the poor rude world
   > Hath not her fellow.
7. **Climax**: A number of phrases or sentences are arranged in ascending order of rhetorical forcefulness. Example from Melville's *Moby Dick*:
   > All that most maddens and torments; all that stirs up the lees of things; all truth with malice in it; all that cracks the sinews and cakes the brain; all the subtle demonisms of life and thought; all evil, to crazy Ahab, were visibly personified and made practically assailable in Moby Dick.
8. **Bathos**: A ludicrous attempt to portray pathos—that is, to evoke pity, sympathy, or sorrow. It may result from inappropriately dignifying the commonplace, elevated language to describe something trivial, or greatly exaggerated pathos.
9. **Oxymoron**: A contradiction in terms deliberately employed for effect. It is usually seen in a qualifying adjective whose meaning is contrary to that of the noun it modifies, such as wise folly.

10. **Irony**: Expressing something other than and particularly opposite of the literal meaning, such as words of praise when blame is intended. In poetry, it is often used as a sophisticated or resigned awareness of contrast between what is and what ought to be and expresses a controlled pathos without sentimentality. This form of indirection avoids overt praise or censure. An early example is the Greek comic character Eiron, a clever underdog who by his wit repeatedly triumphs over the boastful character Alazon.

11. **Alliteration**: The repetition of consonant sounds in two or more neighboring words or syllables. In its simplest form, it reinforces one or two consonant sounds. Example: Shakespeare's Sonnet #12: When I do **c**ount the **c**lock that **t**ells the **t**ime. Some poets have used patterns of alliteration that are more complex by creating consonants both at the beginning of words and at the beginning of stressed syllables within words. For example, Shelley's *Stanzas Written in Dejection near Naples*: The **C**ity's voi**c**e it**s**elf is **s**oft like **So**litude's.

12. **Onomatopoeia**: The naming of a thing or action by a vocal imitation of the sound associated with it, such as *buzz* or *hiss* or the use of words whose sound suggests the sense. A good example is from *The Brook* by Tennyson:
    I chatter over stony ways,
    In little sharps and trebles,
    I bubble into eddying bays,
    I babble on the pebbles.

COMPETENCY 2.0   UNDERSTAND THE MAIN IDEA AND SUPPORTING DETAILS IN WRITTEN MATERIAL

Skill 2.1   Identifying the explicit main idea of a paragraph or passage

The main idea of a passage or paragraph is the basic message, idea, point concept, or meaning that the author wants to convey to you, the reader. Understanding the main idea of a passage or paragraph is the key to understanding the more subtle components of the author's message. The main idea is what is being said about a topic or subject. Once you have identified the basic message, you will have an easier time answering other questions that test critical skills.

Main ideas are either *stated* or *implied*. A *stated main idea* is explicit; it is directly expressed in a sentence or two in the paragraph or passage. An *implied main idea* is suggested by the overall reading selection. In the first case, you need not pull information from various points in the paragraph or passage in order to form the main idea because the author already states it. If a main idea is implied, however, you must formulate, in your own words, a main idea statement by condensing the overall message contained in the material itself.

Skill 2.2   Identifying the statement that best expresses the implied main idea of a paragraph or passage

Practice Question: Read the following passage and select an answer.

Sometimes too much of a good thing can become a very bad thing indeed. In an earnest attempt to consume a healthy diet, dietary supplement enthusiasts have been known to overdose. Vitamin C, for example, long thought to help people ward off cold viruses, is currently being studied for its possible role in warding off cancer and other disease that causes tissue degeneration. Unfortunately, an overdose of vitamin C—more than 10 mg—on a daily basis can cause nausea and diarrhea. Calcium supplements, commonly taken by women, are helpful in warding off osteoporosis. More than just a few grams a day, however, can lead to stomach upset and even kidney and bladder stones. Niacin, proven useful in reducing cholesterol levels, can be dangerous in large doses to those who suffer from heart problems, asthma, or ulcers.

The main idea expressed in this paragraph is

   A.   Supplements taken in excess can be a bad thing indeed.
   B.   Dietary supplement enthusiasts have been known to overdose.
   C.   Vitamins can cause nausea, diarrhea, and kidney or bladder stones.
   D.   People who take supplements are preoccupied with their health.

Answer: Answer A is a paraphrase of the first sentence and provides a general framework for the rest of the paragraph—excess supplement intake is bad. The rest of the paragraph discusses the consequences of taking too many vitamins. Options B and C refer to major details and Option D introduces the idea of preoccupation, which is not included in this paragraph.

Skill 2.3   Recognizing ideas that support, illustrate, or elaborate the main idea of a paragraph or passage

Supporting details are examples, facts, ideas, illustrations, cases, and anecdotes used by a writer to explain, expand on, and develop the more general main idea. A writer's choice of supporting materials is determined by the nature of the topic being covered. Supporting details are specifics that relate directly to the main idea. Writers select and shape material according to their purposes. An advertisement writer seeking to persuade the reader to buy a particular running shoe, for instance, will emphasize only the positive characteristics of the shoe for advertisement copy. A columnist for a running magazine, on the other hand, might list the good and bad points about the same shoe in an article recommending appropriate shoes for different kinds of runners. Both major details (those that directly support the main idea) and minor details (those that provide interesting, but not always essential, information) help create a well-written and fluid passage.

In the following paragraph, the sentences in **bold print** provide a skeleton of a paragraph on the benefits of recycling. The sentences in bold are generalizations, which by themselves do not explain the need to recycle. The sentences in *italics* add details to SHOW the general points in bold. Notice how the supporting details help you understand the necessity for recycling.

While one day recycling may become mandatory in all states, right now it is voluntary in many communities. *Those of us who participate in recycling are amazed by how much material is recycled.* **For many communities, the blue-box recycling program has had an immediate effect.** *By just recycling glass, aluminum cans, and plastic bottles, we have reduced the volume of disposable trash by one third, thus extending the useful life of local landfills by over a decade. Imagine the difference if those dramatic results were achieved nationwide.* **The amount of reusable items we thoughtlessly dispose of is staggering.** *For example, Americans dispose of enough steel everyday to supply Detroit car manufacturers for three months. Additionally, we dispose of enough aluminum annually to rebuild the nation's air fleet. These statistics, available from the Environmental Protection Agency (EPA), should encourage all of us to watch what we throw away.* **Clearly, recycling in our homes and in our communities directly improves the environment.**

Notice how the author's supporting examples enhance the message of the paragraph and relate to the author's thesis noted above. If you only read the boldfaced sentences, you have a glimpse at the topic. This paragraph of illustration, however, is developed through numerous details creating specific images: *reduced the volume of disposable trash by one-third, extended the useful life of local landfills by over a decade, enough steel everyday to supply Detroit car manufacturers for three months, enough aluminum to rebuild the nation's air fleet.* If the writer had merely written a few general sentences, as those shown in bold print, you would not fully understand the vast amount of trash involved in recycling or the positive results of current recycling efforts.

COMPETENCY 3.0 INDENTIFYING A WRITER'S PURPOSE, POINT OF VIEW, AND INTENDED MEANING

Skill 3.1 Recognizing a statement of a writer's expressed or implied purpose for writing (e.g., to persuade, to describe)

An essay is an extended discussion of a writer's point of view about a particular topic. This point of view may be supported by using such writing modes as examples, argument and persuasion, analysis, or comparison/contrast. In any case, a good essay is clear, coherent, well organized, and fully developed.

When an author sets out to write a passage, he/she usually has a purpose for doing so. That purpose may be simply to give information that might be interesting or useful to some reader or other. It may be to persuade the reader to a point of view or to move the reader to act in a particular way. It may be to tell a story, or it may be to describe something in such a way that an experience becomes available to the reader through one of the five senses. Following are the primary devices for expressing a particular purpose in a piece of writing:

- **Basic expository writing** simply gives information not previously known about a topic or is used to explain or define one. Facts, examples, statistics, cause and effect, direct tone, objective rather than subjective delivery, and non-emotional information are presented in a formal manner.

- **Descriptive writing** centers on a person, place, or object, using concrete and sensory words to create a mood or impression and arranging details in a chronological or spatial sequence.

- **Narrative writing** is developed using an incident or anecdote or related series of events. Chronology, the five W's, topic sentence, and conclusion are essential ingredients.

- **Persuasive writing** implies the writer's ability to select vocabulary and arrange facts and opinions in such a way as to direct the actions of the listener/reader. Persuasive writing may incorporate exposition and narration as they illustrate the main idea.

- **Journalistic writing** is theoretically free of author bias. It is essential that it be factual and objective when relaying information about an event, person, or thing. Provide students with an opportunity to examine newspapers and create their own. Many newspapers have educational programs that are offered free to schools.

Skill 3.2 Evaluating the appropriateness of written material for a specific purpose or audience

Tailoring language for a particular **audience** is an important skill. Writing to be read by a business associate will surely sound different from writing to be read by a younger sibling. Not only are the vocabularies different, but the formality/informality of the discourse will also need to be adjusted.

Determining what the language should be for a particular audience, then, hinges on two things: **word choice** and **formality/informality**. The most formal language does not use contractions or slang. The most informal language will probably feature a more casual use of common sayings and anecdotes. Formal language will use longer sentences and will not sound like a conversation. The most informal language will use shorter sentences—not necessarily simple sentences, but shorter constructions—and may sound like a conversation.

In both formal and informal writing, there exists a **tone**, the writer's attitude toward the material and/or readers. Tone may be playful, formal, intimate, angry, serious, ironic, outraged, baffled, tender, serene, depressed, and so on. Both the subject matter and the audience dictate the overall tone of a piece of writing. Tone is also related to the actual words that make up the document, as we attach affective meanings to words, called **connotations**. Gaining this conscious control over language makes it possible to use language appropriately in various situations and to evaluate its uses in literature and other forms of communication. By evoking the proper responses from readers/listeners, we can prompt them to take action.

The following questions are an excellent way to assess the audience and tone of a given piece of writing.

1. Who is your audience? (friend, teacher, business person, someone else)
2. How much does this person know about you and/or your topic?
3. What is your purpose? (to prove an argument, to persuade, to amuse, to register a complaint, to ask for a raise, etc.)
4. What emotions do you have about the topic? (nervous, happy, confident, angry, sad, no feelings at all)
5. What emotions do you want to register with your audience? (anger, nervousness, happiness, boredom, interest)
6. What persona do you need to create in order to achieve your purpose?
7. What choice of language is best suited to achieving your purpose with your particular subject? (slang, friendly but respectful, formal)
8. What emotional quality do you want to transmit to achieve your purpose (matter of fact, informative, authoritative, inquisitive, sympathetic, or angry) and to what degree do you want to express this tone?

Skill 3.3   Recognizing the likely effect on an audience of a writer's choice of words

See Skills 3.2 and 3.4.

Skill 3.4   Using the content, word choice, and phrasing of a passage to determine a writer's opinion or point of view

The **tone** of a written passage is the author's attitude toward the subject matter. The tone (mood, feeling) is revealed through the qualities of the writing itself and is a direct product of such stylistic elements as language and sentence structure. The tone of the written passage is much like a speaker's voice; instead of being spoken, however, it is the product of words on a page.

Often, writers have an emotional stake in the subject, and their purpose, either explicitly or implicitly, is to convey those feelings to the reader. In such cases, the writing is generally subjective; that is, it stems from opinions, judgments, values, ideas, and feelings. Both sentence structure (syntax) and word choice (diction) are instrumental tools in creating tone.

Tone may be thought of generally as positive, negative, or neutral. Below is a statement about snakes that demonstrates this.

>*Many species of snakes live in Florida. Some of those species, both poisonous and non-poisonous, have habitats that coincide with those of human residents of the state.*

The voice of the writer in this statement is neutral. The sentences are declarative (not exclamations or fragments or questions). The adjectives are few and nondescript—*many, some, poisonous* (balanced with *non-poisonous).* Nothing much in this brief paragraph would alert the reader to the feelings of the writer about snakes. The paragraph has a neutral, objective, detached, impartial tone.

Then again, if the writer's attitude towards snakes involves admiration, or even affection, the tone would generally be positive.

>*Florida's snakes are a tenacious bunch. When they find their habitats invaded by humans, they cling to their home territories as long as they can, as if vainly attempting to fight off the onslaught of the human hordes.*

An additional message emerges in this paragraph—the writer quite clearly favors snakes over people. The writer uses adjectives such as *tenacious* to describe his/her feelings about snakes. The writer also humanizes the reptiles, making them brave, beleaguered creatures. Obviously, the writer is more sympathetic to snakes than to people in this paragraph.

If the writer's attitude toward snakes involves active dislike and fear, then the tone would also reflect that attitude by being negative.

> *Countless species of snakes, some more dangerous than others, still lurk on the urban fringes of Florida's towns and cities. They will often invade domestic spaces, terrorizing people and their pets.*

Here, obviously, the snakes are the villains. They *lurk,* they *invade,* and they *terrorize.* The tone of this paragraph might be said to be distressed about snakes.

In the same manner, a writer can use language to portray characters as good or bad. A writer uses positive and negative adjectives, as seen above, to convey the manner of a character.

COMPETENCY 4.0   ANALYZING THE RELATIONSHIP AMONG IDEAS IN WRITTEN MATERIAL

Skill 4.1   Identifying a sequence of events or steps

The ability to organize events or steps provided in a passage (especially when presented in random order) serves a useful purpose, and it encourages the development of logical thinking and the processes of analysis and evaluation.

Working through and discussing examples, such as the one below, with your students helps students to gain valuable practice in sequencing events.

Practice Question: Identify the proper order of events or steps.

1. Matt had tied a knot in his shoelace.
2. Matt put on his green socks because they were clean and complemented the brown slacks he was wearing.
3. Matt took a bath and trimmed his toenails.
4. Matt put on his brown slacks.

Answer: The proper order of events is 3, 4, 2, and 1.

Skill 4.2   Recognizing cause-effect relationships

A cause is the necessary source of a particular outcome. If a writer were addressing the questions, "How will the new tax laws affect small businesses?" or "Why has there been such political unrest in Somalia?" he or she would use cause and effect as an organizational pattern to structure his or her response. In the first case, the writer would emphasize effects of the tax legislation as they apply to owners of small businesses. In the second, he/she would focus on causes for the current political situation in Somalia.

Some word clues that identify a cause-effect passage are *accordingly*, *as a result*, *therefore*, *because*, *consequently*, *hence*, *in short*, *thus*, *then*, *due to* and *so on*.

Sample passage:

Simply put, inflation is an increase in price levels. It happens when a government prints more currency than is already in circulation, and there is, consequently, additional money available for the same amount of goods or services. There might be multiple reasons for a government to crank up the printing presses. A war, for instance, could cause an immediate need for steel. A national disaster might create a sudden need for social services. To get the money it needs, a government can raise taxes, borrow, or print more currency. However, raising taxes and borrowing are not always plausible options.

Analysis: The paragraph starts with a definition and proceeds to examine a causal chain. The words *consequently, reasons,* and *cause* provide the clues.

Explicit Cause and Effect

General Hooker failed to anticipate General Lee's bold flanking maneuver. As a result, Hooker's army was nearly routed by a smaller force.

Mindy forgot to bring the lunch her father had packed for her. Consequently, she had to borrow money from her friends at school during lunch period.

Implicit Cause and Effect

The engine in Lisa's airplane began to sputter. She quickly looked below for a field in which to land.

Luther ate the creamed shrimp that had been sitting in the sun for hours. Later that night, he was so sick he had to be rushed to the hospital.

Skill 4.3 Analyzing relationships between ideas in opposition (e.g., pro and con)

Whenever there are two ideas in opposition, there is the ghost of an "either/or" conceptual basis lurking invisibly in the background of the "pro/con" setting.

For example, one person may argue that automobiles are a safer mode of transportation than are motorcycles and support that contention with statistics showing that fatalities are more frequent per accident in motorcycle crashes than in car crashes.

The opposition to this argument may counter that while fatalities are more frequent per accident in motorcycle accidents, it is erroneous to over generalize from that statistic that motorcycles are "therefore more dangerous."

Thus, each participant in the argument has assumed a position of "either/or," that is to say, the automobile is "either" safer than the motorcycle, "or" it is not (or the motorcycle is "either" safer than the automobile, "or" it is not). With the argument thus formulated, a conclusion acceptable to both sides is not likely to happen. Here is a short essay showing how to avoid this deadlock.

Which is safer—the car or the motorcycle?

Most experienced drivers would agree that while it is more exhilarating to ride a motorcycle than to drive an automobile, it is illogical to therefore conclude that this exhilaration leads to careless driving and, therefore, more accidents, deaths, and injuries to motorcycle riders than car drivers. The critical concept to be understood here is not exhilaration, which is a given, but how the exhilaration comes about and is a cause of serious injury and death of motorcycle riders.

There is safe and unsafe thrill seeking. "Exhilaration" is defined as the "state of being stimulated, refreshed, or elated." An example of safe exhilaration is the excitement of sledding downhill, which results in the sled rider feeling stimulated, refreshed, and/or elated.

Unsafe exhilaration, which is usually the consequence of reckless thrill seeking, is therefore a state of being over-stimulated, frightened, and depressed by terror.

Which then causes exhilaration that is more dangerous, the car or the motorcycle? The answer is that the two forms of exhilaration are the consequences not of the motorcycle or the automobile, per se, but of the operation of the respective vehicles. Without an operator, both vehicles are metal entities, sitting in space, neither threatening nor harmful to anyone.

Therefore, neither the motorcycle nor the car is more or less dangerous than the other is; it is the attitude of their operators that creates the danger, death, and dismemberment resultant from accidents.

Notice how the writer has avoided the logical trap of the "either/or" construction built into the "pro/con" argument by defining the key term "exhilaration" to clarify the issue (and to shift the focus to the operator). He also resolves the either/or dilemma by arguing that it is the operators of the vehicles, not the vehicles themselves, that are responsible for negative consequences.

Skill 4.4   Identifying a solution to a problem presented in a passage

Within the assessment of reading, working with more than one selection is important in deciding if students can generalize. Utilizing the information read to find the answer to a situation presented is the skill. Sometimes this may involve problems specifically identified within what was read. For example, the characters in the story may be having a specific problem, such as a lack of money. Then, as you continue to read the passage, the characters in the story were hired for a new job, which allowed them to earn more money. Using the information read, identify the problem (a lack of money) and the solution (a new job).

In other cases, generalizations will need to be made across multiple selections. In those cases, selecting problems and solutions may be more evasive. Problems and solutions across texts will require broader thinking. The problems and solutions will not be as clearly spelled out in the text. It will involve your thinking on a different level about how the two passages relate. Connecting texts to other texts and finding common elements within them allows you then to draw out the common problems and solutions. Working through multiple selections requires more complex thinking skills and thinking of problems and solutions sometimes in other terms. Perhaps thinking of the challenge or issue that was faced and how that issue was overcome would help to broaden the scope and understanding of identifying the common problem and therefore the solution.

Skill 4.5 Drawing conclusions inductively and deductively from information stated or implied in a passage

An **inference** is sometimes called an *educated guess* because it requires that you go beyond the strictly obvious to create additional meaning by taking the text one logical step further. Inferences and conclusions are based on the content of the passage—that is, on what the passage says or how the writer says it—and are derived by reasoning. Inference is an essential and automatic component of most reading. Examples include making educated guesses about the meaning of unknown words, the author's main idea, or the presence of bias in his or her writing. Such is the essence of inference—you use your own ability to reason in order to figure out what the writer implies. As a reader, then, you must often logically extend meaning that is only implied.

Consider the following example. Assume you are an employer, and you are reading over the letters of reference submitted by a prospective employee for the position of clerk/typist in your real estate office. The position requires the applicant to be neat, careful, trustworthy, and punctual. You come across this letter of reference submitted by an applicant.

> *To Whom It May Concern:*
>
> *Todd Finley has asked me to write a letter of reference for him. I am well qualified to do so because he worked for me for three months last year. His duties included answering the phone, greeting the public, and producing some simple memos and notices on the computer. Although Todd initially had few computer skills and little knowledge of telephone etiquette, he did acquire some during his stay with us. Todd's manner of speaking, both on the telephone and with the clients who came to my establishment, could be described as casual. He was particularly effective when communicating with peers. Please contact me by telephone if you wish to have further information about my experience with Todd.*

Here the writer implies, rather than openly states, the main idea. This letter calls attention to itself because there is a problem with its tone. A truly positive letter would say something such as, "I have the distinct honor of recommending Todd Finley." Here, however, the letter simply verifies that Todd worked in the office. Second, the praise is obviously lukewarm. For example, the writer says that Todd "was particularly effective when communicating with peers." An educated guess translates that statement into a nice way of saying Todd was not serious about his communication with clients.

In order to draw **inferences** and make **conclusions**, a reader must use prior knowledge and apply it to the current situation. A conclusion or inference is never stated. You must rely on your common sense.

Practice Questions: Read the following passages and select an answer.

1.   Tim Sullivan had just turned fifteen. As a birthday present, his parents had given him a guitar and a certificate for ten guitar lessons. He had always shown a love of music and a desire to learn an instrument. Tim began his lessons, and before long, he was making up his own songs. At the music studio, Tim met Josh, who played the piano, and Roger, whose instrument was the saxophone. They all shared the same dream, to start a band, and each was praised by his teacher as having real talent.

From this passage, one can infer that

A. Tim, Roger, and Josh are going to start their own band.
B. Tim is going to give up his guitar lessons.
C. Tim, Josh, and Roger will no longer be friends.
D. Josh and Roger are going to start their own band.

2.   The Smith family waited patiently around carousel number 7 for their luggage to arrive. They were exhausted after their five-hour trip and were anxious to get to their hotel. After about an hour, they realized that they no longer recognized any of the other passengers' faces. Mrs. Smith asked the person who appeared to be in charge if they were at the right carousel. The man replied, "Yes, this is it, but we finished unloading that baggage almost half an hour ago."

From the man's response, we can infer that

A. The Smiths were ready to go to their hotel.
B. The Smiths' luggage was lost.
C. The man had their luggage.
D. They were at the wrong carousel.

Answers:

1. A is the correct choice. Given the facts that Tim wanted to be a musician and start his own band, after meeting others who shared the same dreams, we can infer that they joined in an attempt to make their dreams become a reality.

2. Since the Smiths were still waiting for their luggage, we know that they were not yet ready to go to their hotel. From the man's response, we know that they were not at the wrong carousel and that he did not have their luggage. Therefore, though not directly stated, it appears that their luggage was lost. Choice B is the correct answer.

COMPETENCY 5.0   USING CRITICAL REASONING SKILLS TO EVALUATE WRITTEN MATERIAL

Skill 5.1   Analyzing the stated or implied assumptions on which the validity of an argument depends

On the test, the terms **valid** and **invalid** have special meaning. If an argument is valid, it is reasonable. It is objective (not biased) and can be supported by evidence. If an argument is invalid, it is not reasonable. It is not objective. In other words, one can find evidence of bias.

Practice Questions: Read the following passage and select an answer.

1.   Most dentists agree that Bright Smile Toothpaste is the best for fighting cavities. It tastes good and leaves your mouth minty fresh.

   Is this a valid or invalid argument?

   (A) valid
   (B) invalid

2.   It is difficult to decide who will make the best presidential candidate, Senator Johnson or Senator Keeley. They have both been involved in scandals and have both gone through messy divorces while in office.

   Is this argument valid or invalid?

   (A) valid
   (B) invalid

Answers:

1. It is invalid (B). It mentions that "most" dentists agree. What about those who do not agree? The author is clearly exhibiting bias in leaving out those who disagree.

2. A is the correct choice. The author appears to be listing facts. He does not seem to favor one candidate over the other.

Skill 5.2   Judging the relevance or importance of particular facts, examples, or graphic data to a writer's argument

It is important to assess continually whether or not a sentence contributes to the overall task of supporting the main idea. When a sentence is deemed irrelevant, it is best either to omit it from the passage or to make it relevant by one of the following strategies:

1. Adding detail—Sometimes a sentence can seem out of place if it does not contain enough information to link it to the topic. Adding specific information can show how the sentence is related to the main idea.

2. Adding an example—This is especially important in passages in which information is being argued, compared, or contrasted. Examples can support the main idea and give the document overall credibility.

3. Using diction effectively—It is important to understand connotation, avoid ambiguity, and avoid too much repetition when selecting words.

4. Adding transitions—Transitions are extremely helpful for making sentences relevant because they are specifically designed to connect one idea to another. They can also reduce a paragraph's choppiness.

The following passage has several irrelevant sentences that are highlighted in bold.

The New City Planning Committee is proposing a new capitol building to represent the multicultural face of New City. **The current mayor is a Democrat.** The new capitol building will be on 10th Street across from the grocery store and next to the Recreational Center. It will be within walking distance to the subway and bus depot, as the designers want to emphasize the importance of public transportation. Aesthetically, the building will have a contemporary design, featuring a brushed-steel exterior and large, floor-to-ceiling windows. **It is important for employees to have a connection with the outside world even when they are in their offices.** Inside the building, the walls will be moveable. This will not only facilitate a multitude of creative floor plans, but it will also create a focus on open communication and flow of information. **It sounds a bit gimmicky to me.** Finally, the capitol will feature a large outdoor courtyard full of lush greenery and serene fountains. **Work will now seem like Club Med to those who work at the New City capitol!**

Skill 5.3   Evaluating the logic of writer's argument

An argument is a generalization that is proven or supported with facts. If the facts are not accurate, the generalization remains unproven. Using inaccurate *facts* to support an argument is called a *fallacy* in reasoning. The following are some factors to consider in judging whether the facts used to support an argument are accurate:

1. Are the facts current, or are they out-of-date? For example, if the proposition is, "Birth defects in babies born to drug-using mothers are increasing," then the data must include the latest available.
2. Another important factor to consider in judging the accuracy of a fact is its source. From where was the data obtained, and is that source reliable?
3. The calculations on which the facts are based may be unreliable. It is a good idea to run one's own calculations before using a piece of derived information.

Even facts that are true and have a sharp impact on the argument may not be relevant to the case at hand, as in the following:

1. Health statistics from an entire state may have no relevance, or little relevance, to a particular county or zip code. Statistics from an entire country cannot be used to prove very much about a particular state or county.
2. An analogy can be useful in making a point, but the comparison must match up in all characteristics, or it will not be relevant. Analogies should be used very carefully. They are often just as likely to destroy an argument, as they are to strengthen one.

The importance or significance of a fact may not be sufficient to strengthen an argument. For example, of the millions of immigrants in the U.S., using a single family to support a solution to the immigration problem will not make much difference overall even though those single-example arguments are often used to support one approach or another. They may achieve a positive reaction, but they will not prove that one solution is better than another is. If enough cases were cited from a variety of geographical locations, the information might be significant.

How much is enough? Three strong supporting facts are sufficient to establish the thesis of an argument. However, sometimes many more facts are needed, as in the following example:

Conclusion: All green apples are sour.

- When I was a child, I bit into a green apple from my grandfather's orchard, and it was sour.

- I once bought green apples from a roadside vendor, and when I bit into one, it was sour.
- My grocery store had a sale on green Granny Smith apples last week, and I bought several, only to find that they were sour when I bit into one.

The fallacy in the above argument is that the sample was insufficient. A more exhaustive search of literature, etc., will probably turn up some green apples that are not sour.

Sometimes more than three arguments are too many. On the other hand, it is common to hear public speakers, particularly politicians, who will cite a long litany of facts to support their positions.

A very good example of the omission of facts in an argument is the résumé of an applicant for a job. The applicant is arguing that he/she should be chosen for a particular job. The application form will ask for information about past employment, and unfavorable dismissals from jobs in the past may just be omitted. Employers are usually suspicious of periods when the applicant has not listed an employer.

A writer makes choices about which facts will be used and which will be discarded in developing an argument. Those choices may exclude anything that is not supportive of the point of view the arguer is taking. It is always a good idea for the reader to do some research to spot the omissions and to ask whether they may have an impact on the acceptance of the point of view presented in the argument.

No judgment is either black or white. If the argument seems too neat or too compelling, there are probably facts that might be relevant, which have not been included.

Skill 5.4   Evaluating the validity of analogies

An argument by analogy states that if two things have one thing in common, they probably have other things in common. For example, peaches and plums are both fruits that have chemicals good for people to eat. Both peaches and plums are circular in shape; thus, it could be argued by analogy that *because* something is circular in shape, it is fruit and something good for people to eat. However, this analogical deduction is not logical (e.g., a baseball is circular in shape but hardly good to eat).

An analogy is a comparison of the likenesses of two things. The danger of arguing by analogy rests in a failure to perceive correctly the limitations of the likenesses between the two things compared. Because something is like something else does not make it the same as the compared object or, for that matter, put it in the same class as the original object.

For example, a false argument based on analogical thinking could go like this: "Blake and Blunder are both democrats. Both are married. Both have three children, a dog, and a kitten at home. Therefore, it is likely they will both vote the same way about the school mileage proposal because of their similarities."

This is a false argument by analogy. While the likenesses cited are somewhat striking, these are only likenesses coincidental in nature and not compelling causative roots predictive of behaviors.

However, perceiving the analogical relationship between two things or phenomena is often also the starting point for scientific investigations of reality, and such perceptions are the subjects of a host of scientific theories (e.g., the work of Charles Darwin) and investigations (e.g., wave/particle theories in quantum physics). Such analogical relations require austere scrutiny and analysis, and without such, are essentially meaningless or the stuff of poetic comparisons ("To see the world in a grain of sand"—William Blake).

Thinking in analogies is the way we all began as children to perceive the world and sort it into categories of *good* and *bad* (e.g., "water is a liquid that is good for me; hot oil is a liquid that is bad for me"). Mature writers and thinkers discriminate carefully between all elements of an argument by analogy.

Skill 5.5 Distinguishing between fact and opinion

Facts are verifiable statements. Opinions are statements, such as beliefs, values, judgments, or feelings, which must be supported in order to be accepted, Facts are objective statements used to support subjective opinions. For example, "Jane is a bad girl" is an opinion. However, "Jane hit her sister with a baseball bat" is a *fact* upon which the opinion is based. Judgments are opinions—decisions or declarations based on observation or reasoning—that express approval or disapproval. Facts report what has happened or exists and come from observation, measurement, or calculation. Facts can be tested and verified, whereas opinions and judgments cannot. They can only be supported with facts.

Most statements cannot be so clearly distinguished. "I believe that Jane is a bad girl" is a fact. The speaker knows what he/she believes. However, it obviously includes a judgment that could be disputed by another person who might believe otherwise. Judgments are not usually so firm. They are, rather, plausible opinions that provoke thought or lead to factual development.

Mickey Mantle replaced Joe DiMaggio, a Yankees' centerfielder, in 1952.

This is a fact. If necessary, evidence can be produced to support this.

First year players are more ambitious than seasoned players are.

This is an opinion. There is no proof to support that everyone feels this way.

Practice Questions: Decide if the statement is fact or opinion.

1. The Inca were a group of Indians who ruled an empire in South America.

   (A) fact
   (B) opinion

2. The Inca were clever.

   (A) fact
   (B) opinion

3. The Inca built very complex systems of bridges.

   (A) fact
   (B) opinion

Answers:

1. A is the correct answer. Research can prove this true.
2. B is the correct answer. It is doubtful that all people who have studied the Inca agree with this statement. Therefore, no proof is available.
3. A is the correct answer. As with question number one, research can prove this true.

Skill 5.6   Assessing the credibility or objectivity of the writer or source of written material

Bias is defined as an opinion, feeling, or influence that strongly favors one side in an argument. A statement or passage is biased if an author attempts to convince a reader of something.

Is there evidence of bias in the following statement?

> *Using a calculator cannot help a student understand the process of graphing, so its use is a waste of time.*

Since the author makes it perfectly clear that he does not favor the use of the calculator in graphing problems, the answer is yes, there is evidence of bias. He has included his opinion in this statement.

Practice Question: Read the following paragraph and select an answer.

There are teachers who feel that computer programs are quite useful in helping students grasp certain math concepts. There are also those who disagree with this feeling. It is up to each individual math teacher to decide if computer programs benefit her particular group of students.

Is there evidence of bias in this paragraph?

(A) yes
(B) no

Answer: B is the correct answer. The author seems to state both sides of the argument without favoring a particular side.

"The sky is blue," and "The sky looks like rain"; one is a fact, and the other, an opinion. This is because one is **readily provable by objective empirical data**, while the other is a **subjective evaluation based upon personal bias**. This means that facts are things that can be proved by the usual means of study and experimentation. We can look and see the color of the sky. Since the shade we are observing is expressed as the color blue and is an accepted norm, the observation that *the sky is blue* is therefore a fact. (Of course, this depends on other external factors, such as time and weather conditions.)

This brings us to our next idea—that it looks like rain. This is a subjective observation, in that an individual's perception will differ from another's. What looks like rain to one person will not necessarily look like that to another person. The question thus remains as to how to differentiate fact from opinion. The best and only way is to ask oneself if what is being stated can be proved from other sources, by other methods, or by the simple process of **reasoning**.

Primary and secondary sources

The resources used to support a piece of writing can be divided into two major groups: primary sources and secondary sources.

Primary sources are works, records, etc. that were created during the period being studied or immediately after it. Secondary sources are works written significantly after the period being studied and are based upon primary sources. Primary sources are the basic materials that provide raw data and information. Secondary sources are the works that contain the explications of, and judgments on, this primary material.

Primary sources include the following kinds of materials:

- Documents that reflect the immediate, everyday concerns of people: memoranda, bills, deeds, charters, newspaper reports, pamphlets, graffiti, popular writings, journals or diaries, records of decision-making bodies, letters, receipts, snapshots, etc.
- Theoretical writings that reflect care and consideration in composition and an attempt to convince or persuade. The topic will generally be deeper and have more pervasive values than is the case with "immediate" documents. These may include newspaper or magazine editorials, sermons, political speeches, philosophical writings, etc.
- Narrative accounts of events, ideas, trends, etc., written with intentionality by someone contemporary with the events described
- Statistical data, although statistics may be misleading
- Literature and nonverbal materials, novels, stories, poetry, and essays from the period, as well as coins, archaeological artifacts, and art produced during the period

Secondary sources include the following kinds of materials:

- Books written based on primary materials about the period.
- Books written based on primary materials about persons who played a major role in the events under consideration.
- Books and articles written based on primary materials about the culture, the social norms, the language, and the values of the period.
- Quotations from primary sources
- Statistical data on the period
- The conclusions and inferences of other historians
- Multiple interpretations of the ethos of the time

Guidelines for the use of secondary sources:

- Do not rely upon only a single secondary source.
- Check facts and interpretations against primary sources whenever possible.
- Accept the conclusions of other historians critically.
- Place greatest reliance on secondary sources created by the best and most respected scholars.
- Do not use the inferences of other scholars as if they were facts.
- Ensure that you recognize any bias the writer brings to his/her interpretation of history.
- Understand the primary point of the book as a basis for evaluating the value of the material presented in it to your questions.

COMPETENCY 6.0   APPLYING SKILLS FOR OUTLINING AND SUMMARIZING WRITTEN MATERIALS AND INTERPRETING INFORMATION PRESENTED IN GRAPHIC FORM

Skill 6.1   Organizing information for study purposes (e.g., using note-taking skills, outlining, mapping the text)

Note Taking Skills and Outlines

Being effective note takers requires consistent technique whether the mode of note taking is on 5 X 7 note cards, lined notebook paper, or on a computer. Organizing all collected information according to a research outline will allow the user to take notes on each section and begin the writing process. If the computer is used, then the actual format of the report can be word-processed and information input to speed up the writing process of the final research report. Creating a title page and the bibliography page will allow each downloaded report to have its resources cited immediately in that section.

Note taking involves identification of specific resources that include the author's or organization's name, year of publication, title, publisher location, and publisher. Use the author's last name and page number on cited information when taking notes, whether on the computer or using note cards. In citing information for major categories and subcategories on the computer, create a file for notes that includes summaries of information and direct quotes. When direct quotes are put into a Word file, the cut-and-paste process for incorporation into the report is quick and easy.

In outline information, it is crucial to identify the headings and subheadings for the topic being researched. When researching information, it is easier to cut and paste information under the indicated headings in creating a visual flow of information for the report. In the actual drafting of the report, the writer is able to lift direct quotations and citations from the posted information to incorporate in the writing.

Mapping

Mapping is a strategy that can be used to reach all learning styles, and therefore is an important one to teach. It is exactly what its name implies—a map of the reading. A map helps the reader maneuver through the information in a meaningful manner. Maps can use words with key ideas connected to smaller chunks of information. Teachers can also encourage pictures instead of words to help the visual learner. Adding color to a map can help certain ideas stand out more. This can be particularly helpful for students to begin to understand the process of prioritization in skills. Combining words and pictures is probably the most commonly used type of map. Lines are drawn between connecting concepts to show relationships, and because the reader is creating it himself or herself, it is meaningful. Maps are individual creations and revolve around the reader's learning and prior knowledge.

Skill 6.2   Following written instruction or directions

Step-by-Step

How does one get from here to there, from kindergarten to graduate school or to a trade school? The answer of course is by one step at a time, carefully organizing one's courses of action, with each phase building on the previous step and leading to the next.

Similarly, when taking a test, you are asked to follow written instructions or directions because the examiner wants to see how you manage your answer to the exam question. How do you organize your answer logically? How do you support your conclusions? How well connected are your ideas and the support you bring to your argument?

Look at how the writer does these tasks in the following essay.

Parenting Classes

Someone once said that the two most difficult jobs in the world—voting and being a parent—are given to rank amateurs. The consequences of this inequity are voter apathy and inept parenting, leading to, on the one hand, an apparent failure of the democratic process and, on the other hand, misbehaving and misguided children.

The antidote for the first problem is in place in most school systems. Classes in history, civics, government, and student government provide a kind of "hands on" training in becoming an active member of society so that the step from studenthood to citizenship is clear and expected.

On the other hand, most school systems in the past have avoided or given only lip service to the issue of parenting and parenting skills. The moral issue of illegitimate births aside, the reality of the world is that each year there are large numbers of children born to unwed parents who have had little, or no, training in child rearing.

What was done on the farm in the past is irrelevant here. The farm is gone and/or has been replaced by the inner city, and the pressing issue is how to train uneducated new parents in the child rearing tasks before them. Other issues are secondary to the immediate needs of newborns and their futures, and it is in their futures that the quality of life for all of us is found.

Thus, while we can debate this issue all we wish, we cannot responsibly ignore that uneducated parents need to be educated in the tasks before them, and it is clear that the best way to do this is in the school system, where these new parents are already learning how to be responsible citizens in the civics and other classes currently in place.

Notice how the writer moves sequentially from one idea to the next, maintaining throughout the parallel of citizenship and parenthood, from the opening quotation, paragraph by paragraph to the concluding sentence. Each idea is developed from the preceding idea, each new idea refers to the preceding ideas, and at no point, do related, but irrelevant issues, sidetrack the writer.

Skill 6.3   Interpreting information presented in charts, graphs, or tables

To make a **bar graph** or a **pictograph**, determine the scale to be used for the graph. Then determine the length of each bar on the graph or determine the number of pictures needed to represent each item of information. Be sure to include an explanation of the scale in the legend.

Example: A class had the following grades:
4 A's, 9 B's, 8 C's, 1 D, 3 F's
Graph these on a pictograph and a bar graph.

Pictograph

Grade	Number of Students
A	☺☺☺☺
B	☺☺☺☺☺☺☺☺☺
C	☺☺☺☺☺☺☺☺
D	☺
F	☺☺☺

Bar graph

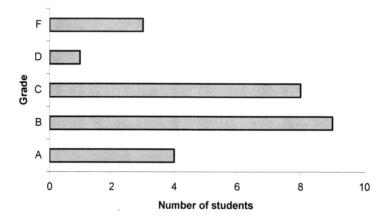

To make a **line graph**, determine appropriate scales for both the vertical and horizontal axes (based on the information to be graphed). Describe what each axis represents, and mark the scale periodically on each axis. Graph the individual points of the graph, and connect the points on the graph from left to right.

Example: Graph the following information using a line graph.

The number of National Merit finalists/school year

	90–91	91–92	92–93	93–94	94–95	95–96
Central	3	5	1	4	6	8
Wilson	4	2	3	2	3	2

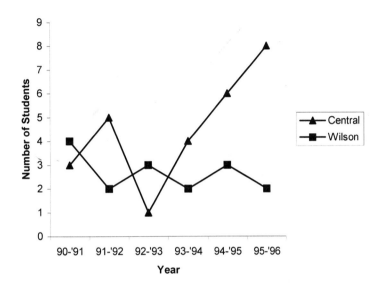

To make a **circle graph**, total all the information that is to be included on the graph. Determine the central angle to be used for each sector of the graph using the following formula:

$$\frac{\text{information}}{\text{total information}} \times 360^{\circ} = \text{degrees in central} \sphericalangle$$

Lay out the central angles to these sizes, and label each section and include its percent.

Example: Graph this information on a circle graph:

Monthly expenses:

Rent, $400
Food, $150
Utilities, $75
Clothes, $75
Church, $100
Misc., $200

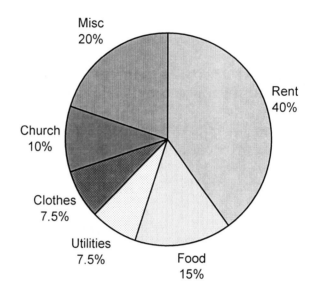

Scatter plots compare two characteristics of the same group of things or people and usually consist of a large body of data. They show how much one variable is affected by another. The relationship between the two variables is their **correlation**. The closer the data points come to making a straight line when plotted, the closer the correlation.

Stem-and-leaf plots are visually similar to line plots. The **stems** are the digits in the greatest place value of the data values, and the **leaves** are the digits in the next greatest place values. Stem-and-leaf plots are best suited for small sets of data and are especially useful for comparing two sets of data. The following is an example using test scores:

4	9
5	4 9
6	1 2 3 4 6 7 8 8
7	0 3 4 6 6 6 7 7 7 8 8 8 8
8	3 5 5 7 8
9	0 0 3 4 5
10	0 0

Histograms are used to summarize information from large sets of data that can be naturally grouped into intervals. The vertical axis indicates **frequency** (the number of times any particular data value occurs), and the horizontal axis indicates data values or ranges of data values. The number of data values in any interval is the **frequency of the interval**.

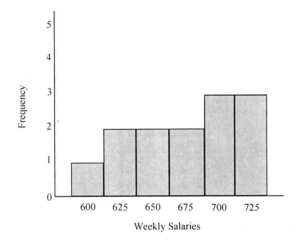

Skill 6.4   Identifying a summary of a passage

Sample Passage

Chili peppers may turn out to be the wonder drug of the decade. The fiery fruit comes in many sizes, shapes, and colors, all of which grow on plants that are genetic descendants of the tepin plant, originally native to the Americas. Connoisseurs of the regional cuisines of the Southwest and Louisiana are already well aware that food flavored with chilies can cause a good sweat, but medical researchers are learning more every day about the medical power of capsaicin, the ingredient in the peppers that produces the heat.

Capsaicin as a pain medication has been a part of fold medicine for centuries. It is, in fact, the active ingredient in several currently available over-the-counter liniments for sore muscles. Recent research has been examining the value of the compound for the treatment of other painful conditions. Capsaicin shows some promise in the treatment of phantom limb syndrome, as well as shingles and some types of headaches. Additional research focuses upon the use of capsaicin to relieve pain in post-surgical patients. Scientists speculate that application of the compound to the skin causes the body to release endorphins—natural pain relievers manufactured by the body itself. An alternative theory holds that capsaicin somehow interferes with the transmission of signals along the nerve fibers, thus reducing the sensation of pain.

In addition to its well-documented history as a painkiller, capsaicin has recently received attention as a phytochemical, one of the naturally occurring compounds from foods that show cancer-fighting qualities. Like the phytochemical sulfoaphane found in broccoli, capsaicin might turn out to be an agent capable of short-circuiting the actions of carcinogens at the cell level before they can cause cancer.

Summary: Chili peppers contain a chemical called capsaicin, which has proved useful for treating a variety of ailments. Recent research reveals that capsaicin is a phytochemical, a natural compound that may help fight cancer.

Outline: -Chili peppers could be the wonder drug of the decade.
              -Chili peppers contain capsaicin.
              -Capsaicin can be used as a pain medication.
              -Capsaicin is a phytochemical.
              -Phytochemicals show cancer-fighting qualities.
              -Capsaicin might be able to short-circuit the effects of carcinogens.

COMPETENCY 7.0   RECOGNIZING PURPOSE AND AUDIENCE

Skill 7.1   Recognizing writing that is appropriate for a given purpose

See Skill 3.1.

Skill 7.2   Recognizing writing that is appropriate for a given audience and occasion

See Skill 3.2.

COMPETENCY 8.0 RECOGNIZING UNITY, FOCUS, AND DEVELOPMENT IN WRITING

Skill 8.1 Recognizing unnecessary shifts in point of view (e.g., shifts from first to third person) or distracting details that impair the development of the main idea in a piece of writing

Point of view defines the focus a writer assumes in relation to a given topic. It is extremely important to maintain a consistent point of view in order to create coherent paragraphs. Point of view is related to matters of person, tense, tone, and number.

Person—A shift in the form that indicates whether a person is speaking (first), is being spoken to (second), or is being spoken about (third) can disrupt continuity of a passage. In your essay, it is recommended that you write in the third person, as it is often considered the most formal of the modes of person. If you do decide to use the more informal first or second person (I, you, or we) in your essay, be careful not to shift between first, second, and third persons from sentence to sentence or paragraph to paragraph.

Tense—Verb tenses indicate the time of an action or state of being—the past, present, or future. It is important to stick largely to a selected tense, though this may not always be the case. For instance, in an essay about the history of environmental protection, it might be necessary to include a paragraph about the future benefits or consequences of protecting the earth.

Tone—The tone of an essay varies greatly with the purpose, subject, and audience. It is best to assume a formal tone for this essay. (See Domain II, Skill 2.3.)

Number—Words change when their meanings are singular or plural. Make sure that you do not shift number needlessly; if a meaning is singular in one sentence, do not make it plural in the subsequent sentence.

Skill 8.2 Recognizing revisions that improve the unity and focus of a piece of writing

Techniques for revising written texts to achieve clarity and economy of expression

Enhancing Interest:

- Start out with an attention-grabbing introduction. This sets an engaging tone for the entire piece, and it will be more likely to pull in the reader.
- Use dynamic vocabulary and varied sentence beginnings. Keep the readers on their toes. If they can predict what you are going to say next, switch it up.

- Avoid using clichés (e.g., as cold as ice, the best thing since sliced bread, nip it in the bud). These are easy shortcuts, but they are not interesting, memorable, or convincing.

Ensuring Understanding:

- Avoid using the words, "clearly," "obviously," and "undoubtedly." Often, things that are clear or obvious to the author are not as apparent to the reader. Instead of using these words, make your point so strongly that it is clear on its own.
- Use the word that best fits the meaning you intend, even if it is longer or a little less common. Try to find a balance, and go with a familiar yet precise word.
- When in doubt, explain further.

Revision of sentences to eliminate wordiness, ambiguity, and redundancy

Sometimes students see this exercise as simply catching errors in spelling or word use. Students need to reframe their thinking about revising and editing. Some questions that need to be asked include:

- Is the reasoning coherent?
- Is the point established?
- Does the introduction make the reader want to read this discourse?
- What is the thesis? Is it proven?
- What is the purpose? Is it clear? Is it useful, valuable, and interesting?
- Is the style of writing so wordy that it exhausts the reader and interferes with engagement?
- Is the writing so spare that it is boring?
- Are the sentences too uniform in structure?
- Are there too many simple sentences?
- Are too many of the complex sentences the same structure?
- Are the compounds truly compounds, or are they unbalanced?
- Are parallel structures truly parallel?
- If there are characters, are they believable?
- If there is dialogue, is it natural or stilted?
- Is the title appropriate?
- Does the writing show creativity, or is it boring?
- Is the language appropriate? Is it too formal? Too informal? If jargon is used, is it appropriate?

Studies have clearly demonstrated that the most fertile area in teaching writing is this one. If students can learn to revise their own work effectively, they are well on their way to becoming effective, mature writers. Word processing is an important tool for teaching this stage in the writing process. Microsoft Word has tracking features that make the revision exchanges between teachers and students more effective than ever before.

Techniques to Maintain Focus

- **Focus on a main point.** The point should be clear to readers, and all sentences in the paragraph should relate to it.

- **Start the paragraph with a topic sentence.** This should be a general, one-sentence summary of the paragraph's main point, relating both back towards the thesis and toward the content of the paragraph. (A topic sentence is sometimes unnecessary if the paragraph continues a developing idea clearly introduced in a preceding paragraph, or if the paragraph appears in a narrative of events, where generalizations might interrupt the flow of the story.)

- **Stick to the point.** Eliminate sentences that do not support the topic sentence.

- **Be flexible.** If there is not enough evidence to support the claim your topic sentence is making, do not fall into the trap of wandering or introducing new ideas within the paragraph. Either find more evidence, or adjust the topic sentence to collaborate with the available evidence.

Skill 8.3   Recognizing examples of well-developed writing

The following example shows good logical order and transitions:

No one really knows how Valentine's Day started. There are several legends, however, which are often told. The first attributes Valentine's Day to a Christian priest who lived in Rome during the third century, under the rule of Emperor Claudius. Rome was at war, and apparently Claudius felt that married men did not fight as well as bachelors. Consequently, Claudius banned marriage for the duration of the war. However, Valentinus, the priest, risked his life to marry couples secretly in violation of Claudius' law. The second legend is even more romantic. In this story, Valentinus is a prisoner, having been condemned to death for refusing to worship pagan deities. While in jail, he fell in love with his jailer's daughter, who happened to be blind. Daily, he prayed for her sight to return, and miraculously it did. On February 14, the day that he was condemned to die, he was allowed to write the young woman a note. In this farewell letter, he promised eternal love and signed at the bottom of the page the now famous words, "Your Valentine."

Sample Prompt and Well-Written Response:

Written on July 15, 1944, three weeks before the Nazis arrested the Frank family, Anne's diary entry explains her worldview and future hopes.

It's difficult in times like these: ideals, dreams, and cherished hopes rise within us, only to be crushed by grim reality. It's a wonder I haven't abandoned all my ideals; they seem so absurd and impractical. Yet I cling to them because I still believe, in spite of everything, that people are truly good at heart.

It's utterly impossible for me to build my life on a foundation of chaos, suffering, and death. I see the world being slowly transformed into a wilderness, I hear the approaching thunder that, one day, will destroy us too, I feel the suffering of millions, and yet, when I look up at the sky, I somehow feel that everything will change for the better, that this cruelty too shall end, that peace and tranquility will return once more. In the meantime, I must hold on to my ideals. Perhaps the day will come when I will be able to realize them!

Using your knowledge of literature, write a response in which you:

- Compare and contrast Anne's ideals with her awareness of the conditions in which she lives; and
- Discuss how the structure of Anne's writing—her sentences and paragraphs—emphasize the above contrast.

Sample Response

This excerpt from The Diary of Anne Frank reveals the inner strength of a young girl who refuses, despite the wartime violence and danger surrounding her, to let her idealism be overcome by hatred and mass killing. This idealism is reflected, in part, by her emphases on universal human hopes, such as peace, tranquility, and goodwill. However, Anne Frank is no dreamy Pollyanna. Reflecting on her idealism in the context of the war raging around her, she matter-of-factly writes, "My dreams, they seem so absurd and impractical."

This indicates Anne Frank's awareness of not only her own predicament, but of human miseries that extend beyond the immediate circumstances of her life. For elsewhere, she writes in a similar vein, "In times like these... I see the world being slowly transformed into a wilderness"; despite her own suffering, she can "feel the suffering of millions."

Yet Anne Frank believes, "in spite of everything, that people are truly good at heart." This statement epitomizes the stark existential contrast of her worldview with the wartime reality that ultimately claimed her life.

The statement also exemplifies how Anne's literary form—her syntax and diction—mirror thematic content and contrasts. "In spite of everything," she still believes in people. She can "hear the approaching thunder...yet, when I look up at the sky, I somehow feel that everything will change for the better." At numerous points in this diary entry, first-hand knowledge of violent tragedy stands side-by-side with belief in humanity and human progress.

"I must hold on to my ideals," Anne concludes. "Perhaps the day will come when I'll be able to realize them!" In her diary, she has done so, and more.

COMPETENCY 9.0   RECOGNIZING EFFECTIVE ORGANIZATION IN WRITING

Skill 9.1   Recognizing methods of paragraph organization

The **organization** of a written work includes two factors: the order in which the writer has chosen to present the different parts of the discussion or argument and the relationships he or she constructs between these parts.

Written ideas need to be presented in a **logical order** so that a reader can follow the information easily and quickly. There are many different ways in which to order a series of ideas, but they all share one thing—to lead the reader along a desired path, while avoiding backtracking and skipping around, in order to give a clear, strong presentation of the writer's main idea. The following are *some* of the ways in which a paragraph may be organized.

Sequence of events—In this type of organization, the details are presented in the order in which they have occurred. Paragraphs that describe a process or procedure, give directions, or outline a given period (such as a day or a month) are often arranged chronologically.

Statement support—In this type of organization, the main idea is stated, and the rest of the paragraph explains or proves it. This is also referred to as relative or order of importance. This type of order is organized in four ways: most to least, least to most, most least most, and least most least.

Comparison-Contrast—The compare-contrast pattern is used when a paragraph describes the differences or similarities of two or more ideas, actions, events, or things. Usually, the topic sentence describes the basic relationship between the ideas or items, and the rest of the paragraph explains this relationship.

Classification—In this type of organization, the paragraph presents grouped information about a topic. The topic sentence usually states the general category, and the rest of the sentences show how various elements of the category have a common base and how they differ from the common base.

Cause-and-Effect—This pattern describes how two or more events are connected. The main sentence usually states the primary cause(s) and the primary effect(s), and their basic connection. The rest of the sentences explain the connection—how one event caused the next.

Spatial/Place—In this type of organization, certain descriptions are organized according to the location of items in relation to each other and to a larger context. The orderly arrangement guides the reader's eye as he or she mentally envisions the scene or place being described.

Example, Clarification, and Definition—These types of organizations show, explain, or elaborate on the main idea. This can be done by showing specific cases, examining meaning multiple times, or describing one term extensively.

Skill 9.2 Reorganizing sentences to improve coherence and the effective sequence of ideas

Paragraphs should contain concrete, interesting information and supporting details to support the main idea or point of view. Fact statements add weight to opinions, especially when the writer is trying to convince the reader of his or her viewpoint. Because every good thesis has an assertion, a well-written passage offers specifics, facts, data, anecdotes, expert opinion, and other details to *show* or *prove* that assertion. While *the author* knows what he or she wants to convey, the *reader* does not.

Like a whole piece of writing, the paragraphs that make up that piece can take a number of forms or combinations of forms. These forms help create an organized and well-structured document:

Cause-and-effect is used to show the reasons for the result of some action.

Compare-and-contrast is used to show similarities and differences between two or more items.

Definition is used if a simple dictionary definition is not sufficient.

Example and illustration is used to show a point by citing examples.

Sequence and process is used to show a step-by-step procedure.

A piece of writing should end with a brief straightforward **concluding paragraph** that ties together the written content and leaves the reader with a sense of its completion. The conclusion should reinforce the main points and offer some insight into the topic, provide a sense of unity for the essay by relating it to the thesis, and signal clear closure of the essay.

Skill 9.3   Recognizing the appropriate use of transitional words or phrases to convey text structure

Even if the sentences that make up a given paragraph or passage are arranged in logical order, the document as a whole can still seem choppy, the various ideas disconnected. **Transitions**, words that signal relationships between ideas, can help improve the flow of a document. Transitions can help achieve clear and effective presentation of information by establishing connections between sentences, paragraphs, and sections of a document. With transitions, each sentence builds on the ideas in the last, and each paragraph has clear links to the preceding one. As a result, the reader receives clear directions on how to piece together the writer's ideas in a logically coherent argument. By signaling how to organize, interpret, and react to information, transitions allow a writer to explain his or her ideas effectively and elegantly.

Logical Relationship	Transitional Expression
Similarity	also, in the same way, just as ... so too, likewise, similarly
Exception/Contrast	but, however, in spite of, on the one hand ... on the other hand, nevertheless, nonetheless, notwithstanding, in contrast, on the contrary, still, yet
Sequence/Order	first, second, third, ... next, then, finally
Time	after, afterward, at last, before, currently, during, earlier, immediately, later, meanwhile, now, recently, simultaneously, subsequently, then
Example	for example, for instance, namely, specifically, to illustrate
Emphasis	even, indeed, in fact, of course, truly
Place/Position	above, adjacent, below, beyond, here, in front, in back, nearby, there
Cause and Effect	accordingly, consequently, hence, so, therefore, thus
Additional Support or Evidence	additionally, again, also, and, as well, besides, equally important, further, furthermore, in addition, moreover, then
Conclusion/Summary	finally, in a word, in brief, in conclusion, in the end, in the final analysis, on the whole, thus, to conclude, to summarize, in sum, in summary

The following example shows good logical order and transitions, with the transition words being highlighted.

No one really knows how Valentine's Day started. There are several legends, **however**, which are often told. The **first** attributes Valentine's Day to a Christian priest who lived in Rome during the third century, under the rule of Emperor Claudius. Rome was at war, and **apparently,** Claudius felt that married men did not fight as well as bachelors. **Consequently**, Claudius banned marriage for the duration of the war. **However,** Valentinus, the priest, risked his life to marry couples secretly in violation of Claudius' law. The **second** legend is **even more** romantic. **In this story**, Valentinus is a prisoner, having been condemned to death for refusing to worship pagan deities. **While** in jail, he fell in love with his jailer's daughter, who happened to be blind. Daily, he prayed for her sight to return, and miraculously it did. On February 14, the day that he was condemned to die, he was allowed to write the young woman a note. **In this farewell letter**, he promised eternal love, and signed at the bottom of the page the now famous words, "Your Valentine."

COMPETENCY 10.0   RECOGNIZING EFFECTIVE SENTENCES

Skill 10.1   Recognizing ineffective repetition and inefficiency in sentence construction

Sentence structure

Recognize simple, compound, complex, and compound-complex sentences. Use dependent (subordinate) and independent clauses correctly to create these sentence structures.

Simple—Consists of one independent clause.
> *Joyce wrote a letter.*

Compound—Consists of two or more independent clauses. The two clauses are usually connected by a coordinating conjunction (and, but, or, nor, for, so, yet). Semicolons sometimes connect compound sentences.
> *Joyce wrote a letter and Dot drew a picture.*

Complex—Consists of an independent clause plus one or more dependent clauses. The dependent clause may precede the independent clause or follow it.
> *While Joyce wrote a letter, Dot drew a picture.*

Compound/Complex—Consists of one or more dependent clauses plus two or more independent clauses.
> *When Mother asked the girls to demonstrate their newfound skills, Joyce wrote a letter, and Dot drew a picture.*

Note: Do **not** confuse compound sentence elements with compound sentences.

> Simple sentences with compound subjects:
> *<u>Joyce</u> and <u>Dot</u> wrote letters.*
> *The <u>girl</u> in row three and the <u>boy</u> next to her were passing notes across the aisle.*

> Simple sentences with compound predicates:
> *Joyce <u>wrote letters</u> and <u>drew pictures</u>.*
> *The captain of the high school debate team <u>graduated with honors</u> and <u>studied broadcast journalism in college</u>.*

> Simple sentence with compound object of preposition:
> *Coleen graded the students' essays for <u>style</u> and <u>mechanical accuracy</u>.*

Types of Clauses

Clauses are connected word groups that are composed of *at least* one subject and one verb. (A subject is the doer of an action or the element that is being joined. A verb conveys either the action or the link.)

Students are waiting for the start of the assembly.
(Subject)   (Verb)

At the end of the play, students wait for the curtain to come down.
                    (Subject)(Verb)

Clauses can be independent or dependent.

Independent clauses can stand alone or they can be joined to other clauses.

Independent clause	for and nor	
Independent clause,	but or yet so	Independent clause

Dependent clauses, by definition, contain at least one subject and one verb. However, they cannot stand alone as a complete sentence. They are structurally dependent on the main clause.

There are two types of dependent clauses: (1) those with a subordinating conjunction, and (2) those with a relative pronoun.

Sample subordinating conjunctions: although, when, if, unless, because

Unless a cure is discovered, many more people will die of the disease.
        (Dependent clause   +   Independent clause)

Sample relative pronouns: who, whom, which, that

The White House has an official website, which contains press releases, news updates, and biographies of the President and Vice-President.
(Independent clause + relative pronoun + relative dependent clause)

Skill 10.2   **Identifying sentence fragments and run-on sentences**

Fragments

Fragments occur (1) if word groups standing alone are missing either a subject or a verb, or (2) if word groups containing a subject and verb and standing alone are actually made dependent because of the use of subordinating conjunctions or relative pronouns.

Error: The teacher waiting for the class to complete the assignment.

Problem: This sentence is not complete because an -ing word alone does not function as a verb. When a helping verb is added (for example, *was*), it will become a sentence.

Correction: *The teacher was waiting for the class to complete the assignment.*

Error: Until the last toy was removed from the floor.

Problem: Words such as until, because, although, when, and if make a clause dependent and thus incapable of standing alone. An independent clause must be added to make the sentence complete.

Correction: *Until the last toy was removed from the floor, the kids could not go outside to play.*

Error: The city will close the public library. Because of a shortage of funds.

Problem: The problem is the same as above. The dependent clause must be joined to the independent clause.

Correction: *The city will close the public library because of a shortage of funds.*

Error: Anyone planning to go on the trip should bring the necessary items. Such as a backpack, boots, a canteen, and bug spray.

Problem: The second word group is a phrase and cannot stand alone because there is neither a subject nor a verb. The fragment can be corrected by adding the phrase to the sentence.

Correction: *Anyone planning to go on the trip should bring the necessary items, such as a backpack, boots, a canteen, and bug spray.*

Fragments are tested in sentences tied to a passage. Items will be in one of two formats.

FORMAT A

Forensics experts conclude that the residents died from chemical <u>radiation. Or</u> perhaps from a mixture of toxic substances and asphyxiation.

A) radiation; or
B) radiation or
C) radiation or,
D) No change is necessary

FORMAT B

<u>Forensics</u> experts conclude that the residents died from chemical <u>radiation. Or</u> perhaps from a mixture of toxic substances and <u>asphyxiation</u>.

A) Forensics
B) radiation or
C) asphyxiation
D) No change is necessary

In each case, you must consider the punctuation between *radiation* and *or*. The punctuation decision is difficult if you do not understand that the second group of words, the one that begins with *Or*, is not a sentence. While these questions may appear to be only about punctuation, they are also about fragments.

The answer in both formats is B. The word group "*Or perhaps from a mixture of toxic substances and asphyxiation*" lacks a subject and a complete verb. It must be joined to the preceding sentence. A comma is not necessary since the word *residents* is the subject of the verb phrase "*died from chemical radiation and of asphyxiation.*"

PRACTICE EXERCISE—FRAGMENTS

→ Choose the option that corrects the underlined portion(s) of the sentence. If no error exists, choose "No change is necessary."

1) Despite the lack of funds in the <u>budget it</u> was necessary to rebuild the roads that were damaged from the recent floods.

   A) budget: it
   B) budget, it
   C) budget; it
   D) No change is necessary

2) After determining that the fire was caused by faulty <u>wiring, the</u> building inspector said the construction company should be fined.

   A) wiring. The
   B) wiring the
   C) wiring; the
   D) No change is necessary

3) Many years after buying a grand <u>piano Henry</u> decided he would rather play the violin instead.

   A) piano: Henry
   B) piano, Henry
   C) piano; Henry
   D) No change is necessary

4) Computers are being used more and more <u>frequently. because</u> of their capacity to store information.

   A) frequently because
   B) frequently, because
   C) frequently; because
   D) No change is necessary

5) Doug washed the floors <u>every day. to</u> keep them clean for the guests.

   A) every day to
   B) every day,
   C) every day;
   D) No change is necessary.

ANSWER KEY: PRACTICE EXERCISE FOR FRAGMENTS

1. B   The clause that begins with *despite* is independent and must be separated with the clause that follows by a comma. Option A is incorrect because a colon is used to set off a list or to emphasize what follows. In Option B, a comma incorrectly suggests that the two clauses are dependent.

2. D   In the test item, a comma correctly separates the dependent clause *After...wiring* at the beginning of the sentence from the independent clause that follows. Option A incorrectly breaks the two clauses into separate sentences, while Option B omits the comma, and Option C incorrectly suggests that the phrase is an independent clause.

3. B   The *phrase Henry decided...instead* must be joined to the independent clause. Option A incorrectly puts a colon before *Henry decided*, and Option C incorrectly separates the phrase as if it was an independent clause.

4. A   The second clause *because...information* is dependent and must be joined to the first independent clause. Option B is incorrect because as the dependent clause comes at the end of the sentence, rather than at the beginning, a comma is not necessary. In Option C, a semi-colon incorrectly suggests that the two clauses are independent.

5. A   The second clause *to keep...guests* is dependent and must be joined to the first independent clause. Option B is incorrect because as the dependent clause comes at the end of the sentence, rather than at the beginning, a comma is not necessary. In Option C, a semi-colon incorrectly suggests that the two clauses are independent.

Run-on sentences and comma splices

Comma splices appear when only a comma joins two sentences. Fused sentences appear when two sentences are run together with no punctuation at all.

Error: Dr. Sanders is a brilliant scientist, his research on genetic disorders won him a Nobel Prize.

Problem: A comma alone cannot join two independent clauses (complete sentences). The two clauses can be joined by a semi-colon or they can be separated by a period.

Correction: *Dr. Sanders is a brilliant scientist; his research on genetic disorders won him a Nobel Prize.*
-OR-
Dr. Sanders is a brilliant scientist. His research on genetic disorders won him a Nobel Prize.

Error: Florida is noted for its beaches they are long, sandy, and beautiful.

Problem: The first sentence ends with the word beaches, and the second sentence cannot be joined with the first. The fused sentence error can be corrected in a few ways: (1) one clause may be made dependent on another with a subordinating conjunction or a relative pronoun, (2) a semi-colon may be used to combine two equally important ideas, or (3) the two independent clauses may be separated by a period.

Correction: *Florida is noted for its beaches, which are long, sandy, and beautiful.*
-OR-
Florida is noted for its beaches; they are long, sandy, and beautiful.
-OR-
Florida is noted for its beaches. They are long, sandy, and beautiful.

Error: The number of hotels has increased, however, the number of visitors has grown also.

Problem: The first sentence ends with the word increased, and a comma is not strong enough to connect it to the second sentence. The adverbial transition *however* does not function the same way as a coordinating conjunction and cannot be used with commas to link two sentences. Several different corrections are available.

Correction: *The number of hotels has increased; however, the number of visitors has grown also.*
[Two separate but closely related sentences are created with the use of the semicolon.]

-OR-

The number of hotels has increased. However, the number of visitors has grown also.
[Two separate sentences are created.]

-OR-

Although the number of hotels has increased, the number of visitors has grown also.
[One idea is made subordinate to the other and separated with a comma.]

-OR-

The number of hotels has increased, but the number of visitors has grown also.
[The comma before the coordinating conjunction *but* is appropriate. The adverbial transition *however* does not function the same way as the coordinating conjunction *but* does.]

PRACTICE EXERCISE—FUSED SENTENCES AND COMMA SPLICES

Choose the option that corrects an error in the underlined portion(s). If no error exists, choose "No change is necessary."

1) Scientists are excited at the ability to clone a <u>sheep however,</u> it is not yet known if the same can be done to humans.

    A) sheep, however,
    B) sheep. However,
    C) sheep, however;
    D) No change is necessary

2) Because of the rising cost of college <u>tuition the</u> federal government now offers special financial assistance, <u>such as loans,</u> to students.

    A) tuition, the
    B) tuition; the
    C) such as loans
    D) No change is necessary

3) As the number of homeless people continues to <u>rise, the major cities</u> like <u>New York and Chicago,</u> are now investing millions of dollars in low-income housing.

    A) rise. The major cities
    B) rise; the major cities
    C) New York and Chicago
    D) No change is necessary

4) Unlike in <u>the 1950s, most</u> households find the husband and wife working full-time to make <u>ends meet in many</u> different career fields.

    A) the 1950s; most
    B) the 1950s most
    C) ends meet, in many
    D) No change is necessary

ANSWER KEY: PRACTICE EXERCISE FOR COMMA SPLICES AND FUSED SENTENCES

1) B   Option B correctly separates two independent clauses. The comma in Option A after the word sheep creates a run-on sentence. The semi-colon in Option C does separate the two clauses but occurs at an inappropriate point.

2) A   The comma in Option A correctly separates the independent clause and the dependent clause. The semi-colon in Option B is incorrect because one of the clauses is independent. Option C requires a comma to prevent a run-on sentence.

3) C   Option C is correct because a comma creates a run-on. Option A is incorrect because the first clause is dependent. The semi-colon in Option B incorrectly divides the dependent clause from the independent clause.

4) D   Option D correctly separates the two clauses with a comma. Option A incorrectly uses a semi-colon to divide the clauses. The lack of a comma in Option B creates a run-on sentence. Option C puts a comma in an inappropriate place.

Skill 10.3   Identifying standard subject-verb agreement

A verb must correspond in the singular or plural form with the simple subject; it is not affected by any interfering elements. Note: A simple subject is never found in a prepositional phrase (a phrase beginning with a word such as of, by, over, through, until).

Present Tense Verb Form

	Singular	Plural
1st person (talking about oneself)	I do	We do
2nd person (talking to another)	You do	You do
3rd person (talking about someone or something)	He She does It	They do

Error: Sally, as well as her sister, plan to go into nursing.

Problem: The subject in the sentence is *Sally* alone, not the word *sister*. Therefore, the verb must be singular.

Correction: *Sally, as well as her sister, plans to go into nursing.*

Error: There has been many car accidents lately on that street.

Problem: The subject *accidents* in this sentence is plural; the verb must be plural also—even though it comes before the subject.

Correction: *There have been many car accidents lately on that street.*

Error: Everyone of us have a reason to attend the school musical.

Problem: The simple subject is *everyone*, not the *us* in the prepositional phrase. Therefore, the verb must be singular also.

Correction: *Everyone of us has a reason to attend the school musical.*

Error: Either the police captain or his officers is going to the convention.

Problem: In either/or and neither/nor constructions, the verb agrees with the subject closer to it.

Correction: *Either the police captain or his officers are going to the convention.*

PRACTICE EXERCISE—SUBJECT-VERB AGREEMENT

Choose the option that corrects an error in the underlined portion(s).
If no error exists, choose "No change is necessary."

1)   Every year, the store <u>stays</u> open late, when shoppers desperately <u>try</u>
        to purchase Christmas presents as they <u>prepare</u> for the holiday.

        A. stay
        B. tries
        C. prepared
        D. No change is necessary.

2)   Paul McCartney, together with George Harrison and Ringo Starr, <u>sing</u>
        classic Beatles songs on a special greatest-hits CD.

        A. singing
        B. sings
        C. sung
        D. No change is necessary.

3)   My friend's cocker spaniel, while <u>chasing</u> cats across the street,
        always <u>manages</u> to <u>knock</u> over the trash cans.

        A. chased
        B. manage
        C. knocks
        D. No change is necessary.

4)   Some of the ice on the driveway <u>have melted.</u>

        A. having melted
        B. has melted
        C. has melt.
        D. No change is necessary.

5)   Neither the criminal forensics expert nor the DNA blood evidence
        <u>provide</u> enough support for that verdict.

        A. provides
        B. were providing
        C. are providing
        D. No change is necessary.

ANSWER KEY: PRACTICE EXERCISE FOR SUBJECT-VERB AGREEMENT

1) D   Option D is correct because *store* is third-person singular and requires the third-person singular verbs *stays*. Option B is incorrect because the plural noun *shoppers* requires a plural verb *try*. In Option C, there is no reason to shift to the past tense *prepared*.

2) B   Option B is correct because the subject, *Paul McCartney,* is singular and requires the singular verb *sings*. Option A is incorrect because the present participle *singing* does not stand alone as a verb. Option C is incorrect because the past participle *sung* alone cannot function as the verb in this sentence.

3) D   Option D is the correct answer because the subject *cocker spaniel* is singular and requires the singular verb *manages*. Options A, B, and C do not work structurally with the sentence.

4) B   The subject of the sentence is *some*, which requires a third-person singular verb *has melted*. Option A incorrectly uses the present participle *having*, which does not act as a helping verb. Option C does not work structurally with the sentence.

5) A   In Option A, the singular subject *evidence* is closer to the verb and thus requires the singular in the neither/nor construction. Both Options B and C are plural forms with the helping verb and the present participle.

Agreements between pronoun and antecedent

A pronoun must correspond to its antecedent in number (singular or plural), person (first, second, or third person) and gender (male, female, or neutral). A pronoun must refer clearly to a single word, not to a complete idea.

A **pronoun shift** is a grammatical error in which the author starts a sentence, paragraph, or section of a paper using one particular type of pronoun and then suddenly shifts to another. This often confuses the reader.

Error:　　A teacher should treat all their students fairly.

Problem:　　Since *teacher* is singular, the pronoun referring to it must also be singular. Otherwise, the noun has to be made plural.

Correction:　*Teachers should treat all their students fairly.*

Error:　　When an actor is rehearsing for a play, it often helps if you can memorize the lines in advance.

Problem:　　*Actor* is a third-person word; that is, the writer is talking about the subject. The pronoun *you* is in the second person, which means the writer is talking to the subject.

Correction:　*When actors are rehearsing for plays, it helps if they can memorize the lines in advance.*

Error:　　The workers in the factory were upset when his or her paychecks did not arrive on time.

Problem:　　*Workers* is a plural form, while *his or her* refers to one person.

Correction:　*The workers in the factory were upset when their paychecks did not arrive on time.*

Error:　　The charity auction was highly successful, which pleased everyone.

Problem:　　In this sentence, the pronoun *which* refers to the idea of the auction's success. In fact, *which* has no antecedent in the sentence; the word *success* is not stated.

Correction:　*Everyone was pleased at the success of the auction.*

Error: Lana told Melanie that she would like aerobics.

Problem: The person that she refers to is unclear; it could be either Lana or Melanie.

Correction: *Lana said that Melanie would like aerobics.*

-OR-

Lana told Melanie that she, Melanie, would like aerobics.

Error: I dislike accounting, even though my brother is one.

Problem: A person's occupation is not the same as a field, and the pronoun *one* is thus incorrect. Note that the word *accountant* is not used in the sentence, so *one* has no antecedent.

Correction: *I dislike accounting, even though my brother is an accountant.*

PRACTICE EXERCISE—PRONOUN/ANTECEDENT AGREEMENT

Choose the option that corrects an error in the underlined portion(s).
If no error exists, choose "No change is necessary."

1) <u>You</u> can get to Martha's Vineyard by driving from Boston to Woods
    Hole. Once there, you can travel over on a ship, but <u>you</u> may find
    traveling by <u>airplane</u> to be an exciting experience.

    A. They
    B. visitors
    C. it
    D. No change is necessary.

2) Both the city leader and the <u>journalist </u>are worried about the new
    interstate; <u>she fears</u> <u>the new roadway</u> will destroy precious farmland.

    A. journalist herself
    B. they fear
    C. it
    D. No change is necessary.

3) When <u>hunters</u> are looking for deer in <u>the woods</u>, <u>you</u> must remain
    quiet for long periods.

    A. they
    B. it
    C. we
    D. No change is necessary.

4) Florida's strong economy is based on the importance of the citrus
    industry. <u>Producing</u> orange juice for most of the country.

    A. They produce
    B. Who produce
    C. Farmers there produce
    D. No change is necessary.

5) Dr. Kennedy told Paul Elliot, <u>his</u> assistant, that <u>he</u> would have to
    finish grading the tests before going home, no matter how long <u>it</u>
    took.

    A. their
    B. he, Paul
    C. they
    D. No change is necessary.

ANSWER KEY: PRACTICE EXERCISE FOR PRONOUN AGREEMENT

1) D   Pronouns must be consistent. As *you* is used throughout the sentence, the shift to *visitors* is incorrect. Option A, *They*, is vague and unclear. Option C, *it*, is also unclear.

2) B   The plural pronoun *they* is necessary to agree with the two nouns *leader* and *journalist*. There is no need for the reflexive pronoun *herself* in Option A. Option C, *it*, is vague.

3) A   The shift to *you* is unnecessary. The plural pronoun *they* is necessary to agree with the noun *hunters*. The word *we* in Option C is vague; the reader does not know to whom the word *we* might refer. Option B, *it*, has no antecedent.

4) C   The noun *farmers* is needed for clarification because *producing* is vague. Option A is incorrect because *they produce* is vague. Option B is incorrect because *who* has no antecedent and creates a fragment.

5) B   The repetition of the name *Paul* is necessary to clarify to whom the pronoun *he* is referring. (It could be Dr. Kennedy.) Option A is incorrect because the singular pronoun *his* is needed, not the plural pronoun *their*. Option C is incorrect because the pronoun *it* refers to the plural noun *tests*.

Skill 10.4   **Identifying standard placement of modifiers, parallel structure, and use of negatives in sentence formation**

Particular phrases that are not placed near the one word they modify often result in misplaced modifiers. Particular phrases that do not relate to the subject being modified result in dangling modifiers.

Error: Weighing the options carefully, a decision was made regarding the punishment of the convicted murderer.

Problem: Who is weighing the options? No one capable of weighing is named in the sentence; thus, the participle phrase *weighing the options carefully* dangles. This problem can be corrected by adding a subject of the sentence capable of doing the action.

Correction: *Weighing the options carefully, the judge made a decision regarding the punishment of the convicted murderer.*

Error: Returning to my favorite watering hole, brought back many fond memories.

Problem: The person who returned is never indicated, and the participle phrase dangles. This problem can be corrected by creating a dependent clause from the modifying phrase.

Correction: *When I returned to my favorite watering hole, many fond memories came back to me.*

Error: One damaged house stood only to remind townspeople of the hurricane.

Problem: The placement of the misplaced modifier only suggests that the sole reason the house remained was to serve as a reminder. The faulty modifier creates ambiguity.

Correction: *Only one damaged house stood, reminding townspeople of the hurricane.*

PRACTICE EXERCISE—MISPLACED AND DANGLING MODIFIERS

Choose the sentence that expresses the thought most clearly and effectively and that has no error in structure.

1)   A. Attempting to remove the dog from the well, the paramedic tripped and fell in also.

      B. As the paramedic attempted to remove the dog from the well, he tripped and fell in also.

      C. The paramedic tripped and fell in also attempting to remove the dog from the well.

2)   A. To save the wounded child, a powerful explosion ripped through the operating room as the doctors worked.

      B. In the operating room, as the wounded child was being saved, a powerful explosion ripped through.

      C. To save the wounded child, the doctors worked as an explosion ripped through the operating room.

3)   A. One hot July morning, a herd of giraffes screamed wildly in the jungle next to the wildlife habitat.

      B. One hot July morning, a herd of giraffes screamed in the jungle wildly next to the wildlife habitat.

      C. One hot July morning, a herd of giraffes screamed in the jungle next to the wildlife habitat, wildly.

4)   A. Looking through the file cabinets in the office, the photographs of the crime scene revealed a new suspect in the investigation.

      B. Looking through the file cabinets in the office, the detective discovered photographs of the crime scene which revealed a new suspect in the investigation.

      C. A new suspect in the investigation was revealed in photographs of the crime scene that were discovered while looking through the file cabinets in the office.

ANSWER KEY: PRACTICE EXERCISE FOR MISPLACED AND DANGLING MODIFIERS

1) B   Option B corrects the dangling participle *attempting to remove the dog from the well* by creating a dependent clause introducing the main clause. In Option A, the introductory participle phrase *Attempting...well* does not refer to a paramedic, the subject of the main clause. The word *also* in Option C incorrectly implies that the paramedic was doing something besides trying to remove the dog.

2) C   Option C corrects the dangling modifier *to save the wounded child* by adding the concrete subject doctors worked. Option A infers that an explosion was working to save the wounded child. Option B never tells who was trying to save the wounded child.

3) A   Option A places the adverb *wildly* closest to the verb *screamed*, which it modifies. Both Options B and C incorrectly place the modifier away from the verb.

4) B   Option B corrects the modifier *looking through the file cabinets in the office* by placing it next to the detective who is doing the looking. Option A sounds as though the photographs were looking; Option C has no one doing the looking.

Faulty parallelism

Two or more elements stated in a single clause should be expressed with the same (or parallel) structure (e.g., all adjectives, all verb forms, or all nouns).

Error: She needed to be beautiful, successful, and have fame.

Problem: The phrase *to be* is followed by two different structures: *beautiful* and *successful* are adjectives and *have fame* is a verb phrase.

Correction: *She needed to be <u>beautiful</u>, <u>successful</u>, and <u>famous</u>.*
(adjective) (adjective)   (adjective)

-OR-

She needed <u>beauty</u>, <u>success</u>, and <u>fame</u>.
(noun)   (noun)   (noun)

Error: I plan either to sell my car during the spring or during the summer.

Problem: Paired conjunctions (also called correlative conjunctions— such as either-or, both-and, neither-nor, not only-but also) need to be followed with similar structures. In the sentence above, *either* is followed by *to sell my car during the spring*, while *or* is followed only by the phrase *during the summer*.

Correction: *I plan to sell my car during either the spring or the summer.*

Error: The President pledged to lower taxes and that he would cut spending to lower the national debt.

Problem: Since the phrase *to lower taxes* follows the verb *pledged*, a similar structure of *to* is needed with the phrase *cut spending*.

Correction: *The President pledged to lower taxes and to cut spending to lower the national debt.*
-OR-
The President pledged that he would lower taxes and cut spending to lower the national debt.

PRACTICE EXERCISE—PARALLELISM

Choose the sentence that expresses the thought most clearly and effectively and that has no error in structure.

1. A. Andy found the family tree, researches the Irish descendents, and he was compiling a book for everyone to read.

    B. Andy found the family tree, researched the Irish descendents, and compiled a book for everyone to read.

    C. Andy finds the family tree, researched the Irish descendents, and compiled a book for everyone to read.

2. A. In the last ten years, computer technology has advanced so quickly that workers have had difficulty keeping up with the new equipment and the increased amount of functions.

    B. Computer technology has advanced so quickly in the last ten years that workers have had difficulty to keep up with the new equipment and by increasing amount of functions.

    C. In the last ten years, computer technology has advanced so quickly that workers have had difficulty keeping up with the new equipment and the amount of functions are increasing.

3. A. The Florida State History Museum contains exhibits honoring famous residents, a video presentation about the state's history, an art gallery featuring paintings and sculptures, and they even display a replica of the Florida Statehouse.

    B. The Florida State History Museum contains exhibits honoring famous residents, a video presentation about the state's history, an art gallery featuring paintings and sculptures, and even a replica of the Florida Statehouse.

    C. The Florida State History Museum contains exhibits honoring famous residents, a video presentation about the state's history, an art gallery featuring paintings and sculptures, and there is even a replica of the Florida Statehouse.

4.   A. Either the criminal justice students had too much practical experience and limited academic preparation or too much academic preparation and little practical experience.

     B. The criminal justice students either had too much practical experience and limited academic preparation or too much academic preparation and little practical experience.

     C. The criminal justice students either had too much practical experience and limited academic preparation or had too much academic preparation and little practical experience.

5.   A. Filmmaking is an arduous process in which the producer hires the cast and crew, chooses locations for filming, supervises the actual production, and guides the editing.

     B. Because it is an arduous process, filmmaking requires the producer to hire a cast and crew and choose locations, supervise the actual production, and guides the editing.

     C. Filmmaking is an arduous process in which the producer hires the cast and crew, chooses locations for filming, supervises the actual production, and guided the editing.

ANSWER KEY: PRACTICE EXERCISE FOR PARALLELISM

1. B   Option B uses parallelism by presenting a series of past tense verbs: *found, researched*, and *compiled*. Option A interrupts the parallel structure of past tense verbs: *found, researches*, and *he was compiling*. Option C uses present tense verbs and then shifts to past tense: *finds, researched*, and *compiled*.

2. A   Option A uses parallel structure at the end of the sentence: *the new equipment and the increased amount of functions*. Option B creates a faulty structure with *to keep up with the new equipment and by increasing amount of functions*. Option C creates faulty parallelism with *the amount of functions are increasing*.

3. B   Option B uses parallelism by presenting a series of noun phrases acting as objects of the verb *contains*. Option A interrupts that parallelism by inserting *they even display*, and Option C interrupts the parallelism with the addition of *there is*.

4. C   In the either-or parallel construction, look for a balance on both sides. Option C creates that balanced parallel structure—*either had...or had*. Options A and B do not create the balance. In Option A, the structure is *Either the students...or too much*. In Option B, the structure is *either had...or too much*.

5. A   Option A uses parallelism by presenting a series of verbs with objects—*hires the cast and crew, chooses locations for filming, supervises the actual production, and guides the editing*. The structure of Option B incorrectly suggests that filmmaking chooses locations, supervises the actual production, and guides the editing. Option C interrupts the series of present tense verbs by inserting the participle *guided*, instead of the present tense guides.

Use of negatives in sentence formation:

Positive	Negative

To Be

Positive	Negative
I <u>am</u> afraid of the dark.	I <u>am not</u> afraid of the dark. (I'm not)
You are going to the store.	You <u>are not</u> going to the store (you're not / aren't)
They <u>were</u> pretty flowers.	They <u>were not</u> pretty flowers. (weren't)
I <u>was</u> enjoying my day off.	I <u>was not</u> enjoying my day off (wasn't)

Conditionals

Positive	Negative
Charlotte <u>will</u> arrive at 8.	Charlotte <u>will not</u> arrive at 8. (won't arrive)
Robert <u>can</u> run 26 miles.	Robert <u>cannot</u> run 26 miles (can't run)
I <u>could have</u> been great!	I <u>could not</u> have been great. (couldn't have)

Present simple

Positive	Negative
I <u>want</u> to go home.	I <u>do not</u> want to go home (don't)
Veronica <u>walks</u> too slowly.	Veronica <u>does not</u> walk too slowly. (doesn't)

Past Simple

Positive	Negative
I <u>skipped</u> rope daily.	I <u>did not</u> skip rope daily. (didn't)

Present Perfect

Positive	Negative
My mom <u>has</u> made my costume.	My mom <u>has not</u> made my costume. (hasn't)
The Thompsons <u>have</u> just bought a dog.	The Thompsons <u>have not</u> just bought a dog. (haven't)

Have Versus Have Got

Positive	Negative
I <u>have</u> 2 sisters.	I <u>do not</u> have two sisters.
I <u>have</u> got 2 sisters.	I <u>have not</u> got two sisters.
Jeremy <u>has</u> school tomorrow.	Jeremy <u>does not</u> have school tomorrow.
Jeremy <u>has</u> got school tomorrow.	Jeremy <u>hasn't</u> got school tomorrow.

Common negative words include:
no, not, none, nothing, nowhere, neither, nobody, no one, hardly, scarcely, barely.

A **double negative** occurs when two forms of negation are used in the same sentence. In order to correct a double negative, one of the negative words should be removed.

Error: I haven't got nothing.

Correction: I haven't got anything.

            -OR-

            I have nothing.

Error: Don't nobody leave until 7 o'clock.

Correction: Do not leave until 7 o'clock.

            -OR-

            Nobody leave until 7 o'clock.

It is also incorrect to combine a negative with an adverb such as "barely," "scarcely," or "hardly."

Error: I can't barely stand it.

Correction: I can't stand it.

            -OR-

            I can barely stand it.

Skill 10.5   Recognizing imprecise and inappropriate word choice

Practice Questions: Choose the most effective word or phrase within the context suggested by the sentences.

1)   The defendant was accused of_____money from his employer.

   A) stealing
   B) embezzling
   C) robbing

2)   Many tourists are attracted to Florida because of its_____climate.

   A) friendly
   B) peaceful
   C) balmy

3)   The woman was angry because the tomato juice left an_____stain on her brand new carpet.

   A) unsightly
   B) ugly
   C) unpleasant

4)   After disobeying orders, the army private was_____by his superior officer.

   A) degraded
   B) attacked
   C) reprimanded

5)   Sharon's critical evaluation of the student's book report left him feeling _____, which caused him to want to quit school.

   A) surprised
   B) depressed
   C) discouraged

6)   The life-saving medication created by the scientist had a very_____impact on further developments in the treatment of cancer.

   A) beneficial
   B) fortunate
   C) miraculous

7) *The Phantom of the Opera* is one of Andrew Lloyd Webber's most successful musicals, largely because of its_____themes.

    A) romantic
    B) melodramatic
    C) imaginary

8) The massive Fourth of July fireworks display_____the partygoers with lots of colored light and sound.

    A) disgusted
    B) captivated
    C) captured

9) Many of the residents of Grand Forks, North Dakota were forced to _____their homes because of the flood.

    A) escape
    B) evacuate
    C) exit

10) The six hundred employees of General Electric were_____by the company due to budgetary cutbacks.

    A) released
    B) terminated
    C) downsized

11) The force of the tornado_____the many residents of the town of Russell, Kansas.

    A) intimidated
    B) repulsed
    C) frightened

12) Even though his new car was a lot easier to drive, Fred_____to walk to work every day because he liked the exercise.

    A) needed
    B) preferred
    C) considered

13) June's parents were very upset over the school board's decision to suspend her from Adams High for a week. Before they filed a lawsuit against the board, they_____with a lawyer to help them make a decision.

A) consulted
B) debated
C) conversed

14) The race car driver's_____in handling the automobile was a key factor in his victory.

A) patience
B) precision
C) determination

15) After impressing the judges with her talent and charm, the beauty contestant_____more popularity by singing an aria from *La Boheme*.

A) captured
B) scored
C) gained

16) The stained-glass window was_____after a large brick flew through it during the riot.

A) damaged
B) cracked
C) shattered

17) The class didn't know what happened to the professor until it was_____by the principal why he dropped out of school.

A) informed
B) discovered
C) explained

ANSWERS: 1.A., 2.C., 3.A., 4.C., 5.C., 6.A., 7.A., 8.B., 9.B. 10. C., 11. C., 12. B., 13. A., 14. B., 15. C., 16. C., 17. C.

COMPETENCY 11.0   RECOGNIZING WRITING THAT CONFORMS TO STANDARDS OF EDITED AMERICAN ENGLISH USAGE

Skill 11.1   Recognizing the standard use of verb forms

Past tense and past participles

Both regular and irregular verbs must appear in their standard forms for each tense. Note: the -ed or -d ending is added to regular verbs in the past tense and for past participles.

Infinitive	Past Tense	Past Participle
Bake	Baked	Baked

Irregular Verb Forms

Infinitive	Past Tense	Past Participle
Be	Was, were	Been
Become	Became	Become
Break	Broke	Broken
Bring	Brought	Brought
Choose	Chose	Chosen
Come	Came	Come
Do	Did	Done
Draw	Drew	Drawn
Eat	Ate	Eaten
Fall	Fell	Fallen
Forget	Forgot	Forgotten
Freeze	Froze	Frozen
Give	Gave	Given
Go	Went	Gone
Grow	Grew	Grown
Have/has	Had	Had
Hide	Hid	Hidden
Know	Knew	Known
Lay	Laid	Laid
Lie	Lay	Lain
Ride	Rode	Ridden
Rise	Rose	Risen
Run	Ran	Run
See	Saw	Seen
Steal	Stole	Stolen
Take	Took	Taken
Tell	Told	Told
Throw	Threw	Thrown
Wear	Wore	Worn
Write	Wrote	Written

Error: She should have went to her doctor's appointment at the scheduled time.

Problem: The past participle of the verb *to go* is *gone*. *Went* expresses the simple past tense.

Correction: *She should have gone to her doctor's appointment at the scheduled time.*

Error: My train is suppose to arrive before two o'clock.

Problem: The verb following *train* is a present tense passive construction, which requires the present tense verb *to be* and the past participle.

Correction: *My train is supposed to arrive before two o'clock.*

Error: Linda should of known that the car wouldn't start after leaving it out in the cold all night.

Problem: *Should of* is a nonstandard expression. *Of* is not a verb.

Correction: *Linda should have known that the car wouldn't start after leaving it out in the cold all night.*

PRACTICE EXERCISE—STANDARD VERB FORMS

Choose the option that corrects an error in the underlined portion(s). If no error exists, choose "No change is necessary."

1) My professor <u>had knew</u> all along that we would pass his course.

    A. know
    B. had known
    C. knowing
    D. No change is necessary

2) Kevin was asked to erase the vulgar words he <u>had wrote.</u>

    A. writes
    B. has write
    C. had written
    D. No change is necessary

3) Melanie <u>had forget</u> to tell her parents that she left the cat in the closet.

    A. had forgotten
    B. forgot
    C. forget
    D. No change is necessary

4) Craig always <u>leave</u> the house a mess when his parents are not there.

    A. left
    B. leaves
    C. leaving
    D. No change is necessary

5) The store manager accused Kathy of <u>having stole</u> more than five hundred dollars from the safe.

    A. has stolen
    B. having stolen
    C. stole
    D. No change is necessary

ANSWER KEY: PRACTICE EXERCISE FOR STANDARD VERB FORMS

1. B   Option B is correct because the past participle needs the helping verb *had*. Option A is incorrect because *it* is in the infinitive tense. Option C incorrectly uses the present participle.

2. C   Option C is correct because the past participle follows the helping verb *had*. Option A uses the verb in the present tense. Option B is an incorrect use of the verb.

3. A   Option A is correct because the past participle uses the helping verb *had*. Option B uses the wrong form of the verb. Option C uses the wrong form of the verb.

4. B   Option B correctly uses the past tense of the verb. Option A uses the verb in an incorrect way. Option C uses the verb without a helping verb such as *is*.

5. B   Option B is correct because it is the past participle. Option A and C use the verb incorrectly.

Inappropriate shifts in verb tense

Verb tenses must refer to the same time consistently, unless a change in time is required.

Error: Despite the increased number of students in the school this year, overall attendance is higher last year at the sporting events.

Problem: The verb *is* represents an inconsistent shift to the present tense when the action refers to a past occurrence.

Correction: *Despite the increased number of students in the school this year, overall attendance was higher last year at sporting events.*

Error: My friend Lou, who just competed in the marathon, ran since he was twelve years old.

Problem: Because Lou continues to run, the present perfect tense is needed.

Correction: *My friend Lou, who just competed in the marathon, has run since he was twelve years old.*

Error: The Mayor congratulated Wallace Mangham, who renovates the city hall last year.

Problem: Although the speaker is talking in the present, the action of renovating the city hall was in the past.

Correction: *The Mayor congratulated Wallace Mangham, who renovated the city hall last year.*

PRACTICE EXERCISE—SHIFTS IN TENSE

Choose the option that corrects an error in the underlined portion(s). If no error exists, choose "No change is necessary."

1) After we <u>washed</u> the fruit that had <u>growing</u> in the garden, we knew there <u>was</u> a store that would buy them.

   A) washing
   B) grown
   C) is
   D) No change is necessary.

2) The tourists <u>used</u> to visit the Atlantic City boardwalk whenever they <u>vacationed</u> during the summer. Unfortunately, their numbers have <u>diminished</u> every year.

   A) use
   B) vacation
   C) diminish
   D) No change is necessary.

3) When the temperature <u>drops</u> to below thirty-two degrees Fahrenheit, the water on the lake <u>freezes</u>, which <u>allowed</u> children to skate across it.

   A) dropped
   B) froze
   C) allows
   D) No change is necessary.

4) The artists were <u>hired</u> to <u>create</u> a monument that would pay tribute to the men who were <u>killed</u> in World War II.

   A) hiring
   B) created
   C) killing
   D) No change is necessary.

5) Emergency medical personnel rushed to the scene of the shooting, where many injured people <u>waiting</u> for treatment.

   A) wait
   B) waited
   C) waits
   D) No change is necessary.

ANSWER KEY: PRACTICE EXERCISE FOR SHIFTS IN TENSE

1) B The past participle *grown* is needed instead of *growing,* which is the progressive tense. Option A is incorrect because the past participle *washed* takes the *-ed*. Option C incorrectly replaces the past participle *was* with the present tense *is.*

2) D Option A is incorrect because *use* is the present tense. Option B incorrectly uses the noun *vacation*. Option C incorrectly uses the present tense *diminish* instead of the past tense *diminished*.

3) C The present tense *allows* is necessary in the context of the sentence. Option A is incorrect because *dropped* is a past participle. Option B is incorrect because *froze* is also a past participle.

4) D Option A is incorrect because *hiring* is the present tense. Option B is incorrect because *created* is a past participle. In Option C, *killing* does not fit into the context of the sentence.

5) B In Option B, *waited* corresponds with the past tense *rushed*. In Option A, *wait* is incorrect because it is present tense. In Option C, *waits* is incorrect because the noun *people* is plural and requires the singular form of the verb.

Skill 11.2   Recognizing the standard use of pronouns

(Refer also to Skill 10.3.)

Rules for clear pronoun references:

Make sure that the antecedent reference is clear and cannot refer to something else.

A "distant relative" is a relative pronoun or a relative clause that has been placed too far away from the antecedent to which it refers. It is a common error to place a verb between the relative pronoun and its antecedent.

Error: Return the books to the library that are overdue.
Problem: The relative clause "that are overdue" refers to the "books" and should be placed immediately after the antecedent.
Correction: Return the books that are overdue to the library.
-or-
Return the overdue books to the library.

A pronoun should not refer to adjectives or possessive nouns.

Adjectives, nouns, or possessive pronouns should not be used as antecedents. This will create ambiguity in sentences.

Error: In Todd's letter, he told his mom he'd broken the priceless vase.
Problem: In this sentence, the pronoun "he" seems to refer to the noun phrase "Todd's letter," though it was probably meant to refer to the possessive noun "Todd's."
Correction: In his letter, Todd told his mom that he had broken the priceless vase.

A pronoun should not refer to an implied idea.

A pronoun must refer to a specific antecedent rather than an implied antecedent. When an antecedent is not stated specifically, the reader has to guess or assume the meaning of a sentence. Pronouns that do not have antecedents are called expletives. "It" and "there" are the most common expletives, though other pronouns can also become expletives as well. In informal conversation, expletives allow for casual presentation of ideas without supporting evidence; however, in writing that is more formal, it is best to be more precise.

Error: She said that it is important to floss every day.
Problem: The pronoun "it" refers to an implied idea.
Correction: She said that flossing every day is important.

Error: They returned the book because there were missing pages.
Problem: The pronouns "they" and "there" do not refer to the antecedent.
Correction: The customer returned the book with missing pages.

Using Who, That, and Which

Who, whom and **whose** refer to human beings and can either introduce essential or nonessential clauses. **That** refers to things other than humans and it is used to introduce essential clauses. **Which** refers to things other than humans and it is used to introduce nonessential clauses.

Error: The doctor that performed the surgery said the man would be fully recovered.
Problem: Since the relative pronoun is referring to a human, who should be used.
Correction: The doctor who performed the surgery said the man would be fully recovered.

Error: That ice cream cone that you just ate looked delicious.
Problem: That has already been used so you must use *which* to introduce the next clause, whether it is essential or nonessential.
Correction: That ice cream cone, which you just ate, looked delicious.

Proper case forms

Pronouns, unlike nouns, change case forms. Pronouns must be in the subjective, objective, or possessive form according to their functions in the sentence.

Personal Pronouns

Subjective (Nominative)		Possessive		Objective	
	Singular	Plural	Singular	Plural	Singular	Plural
1st person	I	We	My	Our	Me	Us
2nd person	You	You	Your	Your	You	You
3rd person	He She It	They	His Her Its	Their	Him Her It	Them

Relative Pronouns
Who	Subjective/Nominative
Whom	Objective
Whose	Possessive

Error: Tom and me have reserved seats for next week's baseball game.

Problem: The pronoun *me* is the subject of the verb *have reserved* and should be in the subjective form.

Correction: *Tom and I have reserved seats for next week's baseball game.*

Error: Mr. Green showed all of we students how to make paper hats.

Problem: The pronoun *we* is the object of the preposition *of*. It should be in the objective form, *us*.

Correction: *Mr. Green showed all of us students how to make paper hats.*

Error: Who's coat is this?

Problem: The interrogative possessive pronoun is *whose*; *who's* is the contraction for who is.

Correction: *Whose coat is this?*

Error: The voters will choose the candidate whom has the best qualifications for the job.

Problem: The case of the relative pronoun *who* or *whom* is determined by the pronoun's function in the clause in which it appears. The word who is in the subjective case, and whom is in the objective. Analyze how the pronoun is being used within the sentence.

Correction: *The voters will choose the candidate who has the best qualifications for the job.*

PRACTICE EXERCISE—PRONOUN CASE

Choose the option that corrects an error in the underlined portion(s). If no error exists, choose "No change is necessary."

1) Even though Sheila and <u>he</u> had planned to be alone at the diner, <u>they</u> were joined by three friends of <u>their's</u> instead.

   A) him
   B) him and her
   C) theirs
   D) No change is necessary.

2) Uncle Walter promised to give his car to <u>whomever</u> will guarantee to drive it safely.

   A) whom
   B) whoever
   C) them
   D) No change is necessary.

3) Eddie and <u>him</u> gently laid <u>the body</u> on the ground next to <u>the sign</u>.

   A) he
   B) them
   C) it
   D) No change is necessary.

4) Mary, <u>who</u> is competing in the chess tournament, is a better player than <u>me</u>.

   A) whose
   B) whom
   C) I
   D) No change is necessary.

5) <u>We, ourselves,</u> have decided not to buy property in that development; however, our friends have already bought <u>themselves</u> some land.

   A) We, ourself,
   B) their selves
   C) their self
   D) No change is necessary.

ANSWER KEY: PRACTICE EXERCISE FOR PRONOUN CASE

1) C   The possessive pronoun *theirs* does not need an apostrophe. Option A is incorrect because the subjective pronoun *he* is needed in this sentence. Option B is incorrect because the subjective pronoun *they*, not the objective pronouns *him* and *her*, is needed.

2) B   The subjective case *whoever*—not the objective case *whomever* —is the subject of the relative clause *whoever will guarantee to drive it safely*. Option A is incorrect because *whom* is an objective pronoun. Option C is incorrect because *car* is singular and takes the pronoun *it.*

3) A   The subjective pronoun *he* is needed as the subject of the verb *laid*. Option B is incorrect because *them* is vague; the noun *body* is needed to clarify *it*. Option C is incorrect because *it* is vague, and the noun *sign* is necessary for clarification.

4) C   The subjective pronoun *I* is needed because the comparison is understood. Option A incorrectly uses the possessive *whose*. Option B is incorrect because the subjective pronoun *who*, and not the objective *whom*, is needed.

5) D   The reflexive pronoun *themselves* refers to the plural *friends*. Option A is incorrect because the plural *we* requires the reflexive *ourselves*. Option C is incorrect because the possessive pronoun *their* is never joined with either *self* or *selves*.

Skill 11.3 **Recognizing the standard formation and use of adverbs, adjectives, comparatives and superlatives, and plural and possessive forms of nouns**

Adjectives are words that modify or describe nouns or pronouns. Adjectives usually precede the words they modify, but not always; for example, an adjective occurs after a linking verb.

Adverbs are words that modify verbs, adjectives, or other adverbs. They cannot modify nouns. Adverbs answer such questions as how, why, when, where, how much, or how often something is done. Many adverbs are formed by adding -ly.

Error: The birthday cake tasted sweetly.

Problem: *Tasted* is a linking verb; the modifier that follows should be an adjective, not an adverb.

Correction: *The birthday cake tasted sweet.*

Error: You have done good with this project.

Problem: *Good* is an adjective and cannot be used to modify a verb phrase such as *have done*.

Correction: *You have done well with this project.*

Error: The coach was positive happy about the team's chance of winning.

Problem: The adjective *positive* cannot be used to modify another adjective, *happy*. An adverb is needed instead.

Correction: *The coach was positively happy about the team's chance of winning.*

Error: The fireman acted quick and brave to save the child from the burning building.

Problem: *Quick and brave* are adjectives and cannot be used to describe a verb. Adverbs are needed instead.

Correction: *The fireman acted quickly and bravely to save the child from the burning building.*

PRACTICE EXERCISE—ADJECTIVES AND ADVERBS

Choose the option that corrects an error in the underlined portion(s).
If no error exists, choose "No change is necessary."

1)   Moving <u>quick</u> throughout the house, the burglar <u>removed</u> several
        priceless antiques before <u>carelessly</u> dropping his wallet.

        A) quickly
        B) remove
        C) careless
        D) No change is necessary.

2)   The car <u>crashed loudly</u> into the retaining wall before spinning <u>wildly</u>
        on the sidewalk.

        A) crashes
        B) loudly
        C) wild
        D) No change is necessary.

3)   The airplane <u>landed</u> <u>safe</u> on the runway after <u>nearly</u> colliding with
        a helicopter.

        A) land
        B) safely
        C) near
        D) No change is necessary.

4)   The <u>horribly</u> <u>bad</u> special effects in the movie disappointed us <u>great</u>.

        A) horrible
        B) badly
        C) greatly
        D) No change is necessary.

5)   The man promised to obey the rules of the social club <u>faithfully</u>.

        A) faithful
        B) faithfulness
        C) faith
        D) No change is necessary.

ANSWER KEY: PRACTICE EXERCISE FOR ADJECTIVES AND ADVERBS

1) A The adverb *quickly* is needed to modify *moving*. Option B is incorrect because it uses the wrong form of the verb. Option C is incorrect because the adverb *carelessly* is needed before the verb *dropping,* not the adjective *careless*.

2) D The sentence is correct as it is written. Adverbs *loudly* and *wildly* are needed to modify *crashed* and *spinning*. Option A incorrectly uses the verb *crashes* instead of the participle *crashing*, which acts as an adjective.

3) B The adverb *safely* is needed to modify the verb *landed*. Option A is incorrect because *land* is a noun. Option C is incorrect because *near* is an adjective, not an adverb.

4) C The adverb *greatly* is needed to modify the verb *disappointed*. Option A is incorrect because *horrible* is an adjective, not an adverb. Option B is incorrect because *bad* needs to modify the adverb *horribly*.

5) D The adverb *faithfully* is the correct modifier of the verb *promised*. Option A is an adjective used to modify nouns. Neither Option B nor Option C, which are both nouns, is a modifier.

Appropriate comparative and superlative degree forms

When comparisons are made, the correct form of the adjective or adverb must be used. The comparative form is used for two items. The superlative form is used for more than two.

	Comparative	Superlative
slow	slower	slowest
young	younger	youngest
tall	taller	tallest

With some words, more and most are used to make comparisons instead of -er and -est.

quiet	more quiet	most quiet
energetic	more energetic	most energetic
quick	more quickly	most quickly

Comparisons must be made between similar structures or items. In the sentence, "My house is similar in color to Steve's," one house is being compared to another house, as understood by the use of the possessive Steve's.

On the other hand, if the sentence reads, "My house is similar in color to Steve," the comparison would be faulty because it would be comparing the house to Steve, not to Steve's house.

Error: Last year's rides at the carnival were bigger than this year.

Problem: In the sentence as it is worded above, the rides at the carnival are being compared to this year, not to this year's rides.

Correction: *Last year's rides at the carnival were bigger than this year's.*

PRACTICE EXERCISE—LOGICAL COMPARISONS

Choose the sentence that logically and correctly expresses the comparison.

1) A. This year's standards are higher than last year.
    B. This year's standards are more high than last year.
    C. This year's standards are higher than last year's.

2) A. Tom's attitudes are very different from his father's.
    B. Toms attitudes are very different from his father.
    C. Tom's attitudes are very different from his father.

3) A. John is the stronger member of the gymnastics team.
    B. John is the strongest member of the gymnastics team.
    C. John is the most strong member of the gymnastics team.

4) A. Tracy's book report was longer than Tony's.
    B. Tracy's book report was more long than Tony's.
    C. Tracy's book report was longer than Tony.

5) A. Becoming a lawyer is as difficult as, if not more difficult than, becoming a doctor.

    B. Becoming a lawyer is as difficult, if not more difficult than, becoming a doctor.

    C. Becoming a lawyer is difficult, if not more difficult than, becoming a doctor.

6) A. Better than any movie of the modern era, *Schindler's List* portrays the destructiveness of hate.

    B. More better than any movie of the modern era, *Schindler's List* portrays the destructiveness of hate.

    C. Better than any other movie of the modern era, *Schindler's List* portrays the destructiveness of hate.

ANSWER KEY: PRACTICE EXERCISE FOR LOGICAL COMPARISONS

1) C   Option C is correct because the comparison is between this year's standards and last year's [standards is understood]. Option A compares the standards to last year. In Option B, the faulty comparative *more high* should be *higher*.

2) A   Option A is incorrect because Tom's attitudes are compared to his father's [attitudes is understood]. Option B deletes the necessary apostrophe to show possession (Tom's), and the comparison is faulty with *attitudes* compared to father. While Option C uses the correct possessive, it retains the faulty comparison shown in Option B.

3) B   In Option B, John is correctly the strongest member of a team that consists of more than two people. Option A uses the comparative *stronger* (comparison of two items) rather than the superlative *strongest* (comparison of more than two). Option C uses a faulty superlative, *most strong*.

4) A   Option A is correct because the comparison is between Tracy's book report and Tony's (book report). Option B uses the faulty comparative *more long* instead of longer. Option C wrongly compares Tracy's book report to Tony.

5) A   In Option A, the dual comparison is correctly stated: *as difficult as, if not more difficult than*. Remember to test the dual comparison by taking out the intervening comparison. Option B deletes the necessary *as* after the first *difficult*. Option C deletes the *as* before and after the first *difficult*.

6) C   Option C includes the necessary word *other* in the comparison *better than any other movie*. The comparison in Option A is not complete, and Option B uses a faulty comparative *more better*.

Plural nouns

A good dictionary should replace the multiplicity and complexity of spelling rules based on phonics, letter doubling, and exceptions to rules not mastered by adulthood. As spelling mastery is also difficult for adolescents, our recommendation is the same. Learning the use of a dictionary and thesaurus will be a more rewarding use of time.

Most plurals of nouns that end in hard consonants or hard consonant sounds followed by a silent *e* are made by adding *-s*. Some words ending in vowels only add *-s*.

fingers, numerals, banks, bugs, riots, homes, gates, radios, bananas

Nouns that end in soft consonant sounds *s, j, x, z, ch,* and *sh,* add *-es*. Some nouns ending in *o* add *-es*.

dresses, waxes, churches, brushes, tomatoes

Nouns ending in *y* preceded by a vowel just add *-s*.

boys, alleys

Nouns ending in *y* preceded by a consonant change the *y* to *i* and add *-es*.

babies, corollaries, frugalities, poppies

Some nouns' plurals are formed irregularly or remain the same.

sheep, deer, children, leaves, oxen

Some nouns derived from foreign words, especially Latin, may make their plurals in two different ways—one of them Anglicized. Sometimes, the meanings are the same; other times, the two plurals are used in slightly different contexts. It is always wise to consult the dictionary.

appendices, appendixes   criterion, criteria
indexes, indices   crisis, crises

Make the plurals of closed (solid) compound words in the usual way except for words ending in *–ful,* which make their plurals on the root word.

timelines, hairpins

Make the plurals of open or hyphenated compounds by adding the change in inflection to the word that changes in number.

> fathers-in-law, courts-martial, masters of art, doctors of medicine

Make the plurals of letters, numbers, and abbreviations by adding -*s*.

> fives and tens, IBMs, 1990s, *p*s and *q*s (Note that letters are italicized.)

Possessive nouns

Make the possessives of singular nouns by adding an apostrophe followed by the letter *s* (*'s*).

> baby's bottle, father's job, elephant's eye, teacher's desk, sympathizer's protests, week's postponement

Make the possessive of singular nouns ending in *s* by adding either an apostrophe or an (*'s*) depending upon common usage or sound. When making the possessive causes difficulty, use a prepositional phrase instead. Even with the sibilant ending, with a few exceptions, it is advisable to use the (*'s*) construction.

> dress's color, species' characteristics or characteristics of the species, James' hat or James's hat, Delores's shirt.

Make the possessive of plural nouns ending in *s* by adding the apostrophe after the *s*.

> horses' coats, jockeys' times, four days' time

Make possessives of plural nouns that do not end in *s* the same as singular nouns by adding *'s*.

> children's shoes, deer's antlers, cattle's horns

Make possessives of compound nouns by adding the inflection at the end of the word or phrase.

> the mayor of Los Angeles' campaign, the mailman's new truck, the mailmen's new trucks, my father-in-law's first wife, the keepsakes' values, several daughters-in-law's husbands

Note: Because a gerund functions as a noun, any noun preceding it and operating as a possessive adjective must reflect the necessary inflection.

However, if the gerundive following the noun is a participle, no inflection is added.

> The general was perturbed by the private's sleeping on duty. (The word *sleeping* is a gerund, the object of the preposition *by.*
> > *-but-*
> The general was perturbed to see the private sleeping on duty. (The word *sleeping* is a participle modifying *private.*)

Skill 11.4   Recognizing standard punctuation

Commas

Commas indicate a brief pause. They are used to set off dependent clauses and long introductory word groups, to separate words in a series, to set off unimportant material that interrupts the flow of the sentence, and to separate independent clauses joined by conjunctions.

Error: After I finish my master's thesis I plan to work in Chicago.

Problem: A comma is needed after an introductory dependent word group containing a subject and verb.

Correction: *After I finish my master's thesis, I plan to work in Chicago.*

Error: I washed waxed and vacuumed my car today.

Problem: Commas should separate nouns, phrases, or clauses in a list, as well as two or more coordinate adjectives that modify one word. Although the word *and* is sometimes considered optional, it is often necessary to clarify the meaning.

Correction: *I washed, waxed, and vacuumed my car today.*

Error: She was a talented dancer but she is mostly remembered for her singing ability.

Problem: A comma is needed before a conjunction that joins two independent clauses (complete sentences).

Correction: *She was a talented dancer, but she is mostly remembered for her singing ability.*

Semicolons and colons

Semicolons are needed to separate two or more closely related independent clauses when the second clause is introduced by a transitional adverb. (These clauses may also be written as separate sentences, preferably by placing the adverb within the second sentence). **Colons** are used to introduce lists and to emphasize what follows.

Error: I climbed to the top of the mountain, it took me three hours.

Problem: A comma alone cannot separate two independent clauses. Instead, a semicolon is needed to separate two related sentences.

Correction: *I climbed to the top of the mountain; it took me three hours.*

Error: In the movie, asteroids destroyed Dallas, Texas, Kansas City, Missouri, and Boston, Massachusetts.

Problem: Semicolons are needed to separate items in a series that already contain internal punctuation.

Correction: *In the movie, asteroids destroyed Dallas, Texas; Kansas City, Missouri; and Boston, Massachusetts.*

Error: Essays will receive the following grades; A for excellent, B for good, C for average, and D for unsatisfactory.

Problem: A colon is needed to emphasize the information or list that follows.

Correction: *Essays will receive the following grades: A for excellent, B for good, C for average, and D for unsatisfactory.*

Error: The school carnival included: amusement rides, clowns, food booths, and a variety of games.

Problem: The material preceding the colon and the list that follows is not a complete sentence. Do not separate a verb (or preposition) from the object.

Correction: *The school carnival included amusement rides, clowns, food booths, and a variety of games.*

Apostrophes

Apostrophes are used to show either contractions or possession.

Error: She shouldnt be permitted to smoke cigarettes in the building.

Problem: An apostrophe is needed in a contraction in place of the missing letter.

Correction: *She shouldn't be permitted to smoke cigarettes in the building.*

Error: My cousins motorcycle was stolen from his driveway.

Problem: An apostrophe is needed to show possession.

Correction: *My cousin's motorcycle was stolen from his driveway.*
(Note: The use of the apostrophe before the letter "s" means that there is just one cousin. The plural form would read the following way: My cousins' motorcycle was stolen from their driveway.)

Error: The childrens new kindergarten teacher was also a singer.

Problem: An apostrophe is needed to show possession.

Correction: *The children's' new kindergarten teacher was also a singer.*

Error: Children screams could be heard for miles.

Problem: An apostrophe and the letter *s* are needed in the sentence to show whose screams they are.

Correction: *Children's screams could be heard for miles.*
(Note: Because the word children is already plural, the apostrophe and *s* must be added afterward to show ownership.)

Quotation marks

In a quoted statement that is either declarative or imperative, place the period inside the closing quotation marks.

"The airplane crashed on the runway during takeoff."

If the quotation is followed by other words in the sentence, place a comma inside the closing quotations marks and a period at the end of the sentence.

"The airplane crashed on the runway during takeoff," said the announcer.

In most instances in which a quoted title or expression occurs at the end of a sentence, the period is placed before either the single or double quotation marks.

"The middle school readers were unprepared to understand Bryant's poem 'Thanatopsis.'"

Early book-length adventure stories such as *Don Quixote* and *The Three Musketeers* were known as "picaresque novels."

The final quotation mark would precede the period if the content of the sentence were about a speech or quote so that the understanding of the meaning would be confused by the placement of the period.

The first thing out of his mouth was, "Hi, I'm home."
-but-
The first line of his speech began, "I arrived home to an empty house".

In sentences that are interrogatory or exclamatory, the question mark or exclamation point should be positioned outside the closing quotation marks if the quote itself is a statement or command or cited title.

Who decided to lead us in the recitation of the "Pledge of Allegiance"?

Why was Tillie shaking as she began her recitation, "Once upon a midnight dreary..."?

I was embarrassed when Mrs. White said, "Your slip is showing"!

In sentences that are declarative, but the quotation is a question or an exclamation, place the question mark or exclamation point inside the quotation marks.

The hall monitor yelled, "Fire! Fire!"

"Fire! Fire!" yelled the hall monitor.

Cory shrieked, "Is there a mouse in the room?" (In this instance, the question supersedes the exclamation.)

Quotations—whether words, phrases, or clauses—should be punctuated according to the rules of the grammatical function they serve in the sentence.

The works of Shakespeare, "the bard of Avon," have been contested as originating with other authors.

"You'll get my money," the old man warned, "when 'Hell freezes over'."

Sheila cited the passage that began "Four score and seven years ago...." (Note the ellipsis followed by an enclosed period.)

"Old Ironsides" inspired the preservation of the U. S. S. Constitution.

Use quotation marks to enclose the titles of shorter works: songs, short poems, short stories, essays, and chapters of books. (See "Using Italics" for punctuating longer titles.)

"The Tell-Tale Heart"   "Casey at the Bat"   "America the Beautiful"

Dashes and Italics

Place **dashes** to denote sudden breaks in thought.

> Some periods in literature—the Romantic Age, for example—
> spanned different periods in different countries.

Use dashes instead of commas if commas are already used elsewhere in the sentence for amplification or explanation.

> The Fireside Poets included three Brahmans—James Russell
> Lowell, Henry David Wadsworth, Oliver Wendell Holmes—
> and John Greenleaf Whittier.

Use **italics** to punctuate the titles of long works of literature, names of periodical publications, musical scores, works of art and motion picture television, and radio programs. (When unable to write in italics, students should be instructed to underline in their own writing where italics would be appropriate.)

> *The Idylls of the King*   *Hiawatha*   *The Sound and the Fury*
> *Mary Poppins*   *Newsweek*   *The Nutcracker Suite*

Capitalize all proper names of persons (including specific organizations or agencies of government); places (countries, states, cities, parks, and specific geographical areas); and things (political parties, structures, historical and cultural terms, and calendar and time designations); and religious terms (any deity, revered person or group, sacred writings).

> Percy Bysshe Shelley, Argentina, Mount Rainier National Park,
> Grand Canyon, League of Nations, the Sears Tower, Birmingham,
> Lyric Theater, Americans, Midwesterners, Democrats, Renaissance,
> Boy Scouts of America, Easter, God, Bible, Dead Sea Scrolls, Koran

Capitalize proper adjectives and titles used with proper names.

California Gold Rush, President John Adams, French fries, Homeric epic, Romanesque architecture, Senator John Glenn

Note: Some words that represent titles and offices are not capitalized unless used with a proper name.

Capitalized	Not Capitalized
Congressman McKay	the congressman from Florida
Commander Alger	commander of the Pacific Fleet
Queen Elizabeth	the queen of England

Capitalize all main words in titles of works of literature, art, and music.

Error: Emma went to Dr. Peters for treatment since her own Doctor was on vacation.

Problem: The use of capital letters with Emma and Dr .Peters is correct since they are specific (proper) names; the title Dr. is also capitalized. However, the word *doctor* is not a specific name and should not be capitalized.

Correction: *Emma went to Dr. Peters for treatment since her own doctor was on vacation.*

Error: Our Winter Break does not start until next wednesday.

Problem: Days of the week are capitalized, but seasons are not capitalized.

Correction: *Our winter break does not start until next Wednesday.*

Error: The exchange student from israel, who came to study Biochemistry, spoke spanish very well.

Problem: Languages and the names of countries are always capitalized. Courses are also capitalized when they refer to a specific course; they are not capitalized when they refer to courses in general.

Correction: *The exchange student from Israel, who came to study Biochemistry, spoke Spanish very well.*

DOMAIN III.   ESSAY

This section of the writing subtest consists of one writing assignment. The assignment can be found on the next page. You are asked to prepare a multiple-paragraph composition of approximately 300 to 600 words on an assigned topic.

Your composition should effectively communicate a whole message to the specified audience for the stated purpose. You will be assessed on your ability to express, organize, and support opinions and ideas. You will not be assessed on the position you express. You will be asked to:

- Demonstrate the ability to write on a given topic using language and style appropriate to a given audience, purpose, and occasion.
- Demonstrate the ability to prepare a unified and focused piece of writing.
- Demonstrate the ability to develop and support a topic in a piece of writing.
- Demonstrate the ability to prepare a well-organized piece of writing.
- Demonstrate the ability to use effective sentence structure.
- Demonstrate the ability to apply the standards of edited American English usage.
- Demonstrate the ability to spell, capitalize, and punctuate according to the standards of edited American English.

Your composition will be evaluated based on the following criteria:

APPROPRIATENESS: The extent to which the response addresses the topic and uses language and style appropriate to the given audience, purpose, and occasion

MECHANICAL CONVENTIONS: The extent to which words are spelled correctly and to which the response follows the conventions of punctuation and capitalization

USAGE: The extent to which the writing shows care and precision in word choice and is free of usage errors

SENTENCE STRUCTURE: The effectiveness of the sentence structure and the extent to which the sentences are free of structural errors

FOCUS AND UNITY: The clarity with which the response states and maintains focus on the main idea or point of view

ORGANIZATION: The clarity of the writing and the logical sequence of ideas

DEVELOPMENT: The extent to which the response provides statements of appropriate depth, specificity, and/or accuracy

ESSAY GUIDELINES

Even before you select a topic, determine what each prompt is asking you to discuss. This first decision is crucial. If you pick a topic you do not really understand or about which you have little to say, you will have difficulty developing your essay. So take a few moments to analyze each topic carefully *before* you begin to write.

Topic A: A modern invention that can be considered a wonder of the world

In general, the topic prompts have two parts:
- the *SUBJECT* of the topic and
- an *ASSERTION* about the subject.

The **subject** is *a modern invention*. In this prompt, the word *modern* indicates you should discuss something invented recently, at least in this century. The word *invention* indicates you are to write about something created by humans (not natural phenomena such as mountains or volcanoes). You may discuss an invention that has potential for harm, such as chemical warfare or the atomic bomb; or you may discuss an invention that has the potential for good, such as the computer, DNA testing, television, antibiotics, and so on.

The **assertion** (a statement of point of view) is that *the invention has such powerful or amazing qualities that it should be considered a wonder of the world.* The assertion states your point of view about the subject, and it limits the range for discussion. In other words, you would discuss particular qualities or uses of the invention, not just discuss how it was invented or whether it should have been invented at all.

Note also that this particular topic encourages you to use examples to show the reader that a particular invention is a modern wonder. Some topic prompts lend themselves to essays with an argumentative edge, one in which you take a stand on a particular issue and persuasively prove your point. Here, you undoubtedly could offer examples or illustrations of the many "wonders" and uses of the particular invention you chose.

Be aware that misreading or misinterpreting the topic prompt can lead to serious problems. Papers that do not address the topic occur when one reads too quickly or only half understands the topic. This may happen if you misread or misinterpret words. Misreading can also lead to a paper that addresses only part of the topic prompt rather than the entire topic.

To develop a complete essay, spend a few minutes planning. Jot down your ideas, and quickly sketch an outline. Although you may feel under pressure to begin writing, you will write more effectively if you plan your major points.

Prewriting

Before actually writing, you will need to generate content and to develop a writing plan. Three prewriting techniques that can be helpful are:

Brainstorming

When brainstorming, quickly create a list of words and ideas that are connected to the topic. Let your mind roam free to generate as many relevant ideas as possible in a few minutes. For example, on the topic of computers, you may write:

      computer—modern invention
      types—personal computers, microchips in calculators and watches
      wonder—acts like an electronic brain
      uses—science, medicine, offices, homes, schools
      problems—too much reliance; the machines are not perfect

This list could help you focus on the topic and state the points you could develop in the body paragraphs. The brainstorming list keeps you on track and is well worth the few minutes it takes to jot down the ideas. While you have not ordered the ideas, seeing them on paper is an important step.

Questioning

Questioning helps you focus as you mentally ask a series of exploratory questions about the topic. You may use the most basic questions: **who, what, where, when, why, and how.**

"**What** is my subject?"
    [computers]

"**What** types of computers are there?"
    [personal computers, microchip computers]

"**Why** have computers been a positive invention?"
    [act like an electronic brain in machinery and equipment; help solve complex scientific problems]

"**How** have computers been a positive invention?"
    [used to make improvements in]
- science (space exploration, moon landings)
- medicine (MRIs, CT scans, surgical tools, research models)
- business (PCs, FAX, telephone equipment)
- education (computer programs for math, languages, science, social studies), and
- personal use (family budgets, tax programs, healthy diet plans)]

"How can I show that computers are good?"
    [cite numerous examples]

"What problems do I see with computers?"
    [too much reliance; not yet perfect]

"What personal experiences would help me develop examples to respond to this topic?
    [my own experiences using computers]

Of course, you may not have time to write out the questions completely. You might just write the words *who, what, where, why,* and *how* and the major points next to each. An abbreviated list might look as follows:

What—computers/modern wonder/making life better
How—through technological improvements: lasers, calculators, CT scans, MRIs.
Where—in science and space exploration, medicine, schools, offices

In a few moments, your questions should help you to focus on the topic and to generate interesting ideas and points to make in the essay. Later in the writing process, you can look back at the list to be sure you have made the key points you intended.

Clustering

Some visual thinkers find clustering to be an effective prewriting method. When clustering, you draw a box in the center of your paper and write your topic within that box. Then, you draw lines from the center box and connect it to small satellite boxes that contain related ideas. Note the cluster below on computers:

SAMPLE CLUSTER

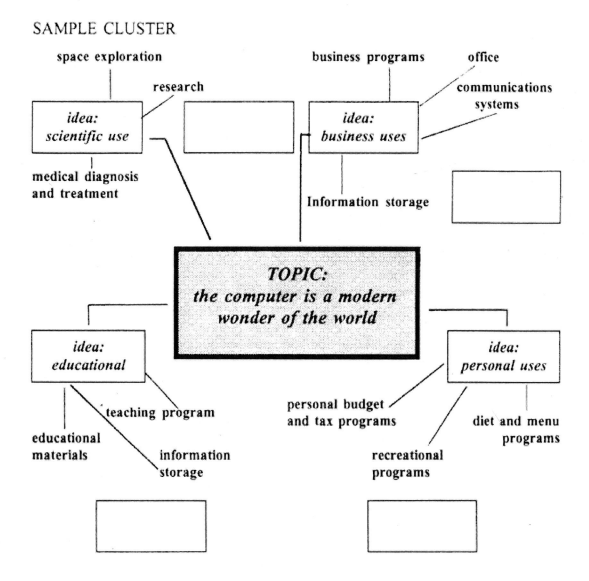

Writing the Thesis

After focusing on the topic and generating your ideas, form your thesis, the controlling idea of your essay. The thesis is your general statement to the reader that expresses your point of view and guides your essay's purpose and scope. The thesis should allow you either to explain your subject or to take an arguable position about it. A strong thesis statement is neither too narrow nor too broad.

Subject and Assertion of the Thesis

From the analysis of the general topic, you saw the topic in terms of its two parts: *subject* and *assertion*. On the exam, your thesis or viewpoint on a particular topic is stated in two important points:

1.   The *SUBJECT* of the paper
2.   The *ASSERTION* about the subject

The **subject of the thesis** relates directly to the topic prompt but expresses the specific area you have chosen to discuss. (Remember, the exam topic will be general and will allow you to choose a particular subject related to the topic.) For example, the computer is one modern invention.

The **assertion of the thesis** is your viewpoint, or opinion, about the subject. The assertion provides the motive or purpose for your essay, and it may be an arguable point or one that explains or illustrates a point of view.

For example, you may present an argument for or against a particular issue. You may contrast two people, objects, or methods to show that one is better than the other is. You may analyze a situation in all aspects and make recommendations for improvement. You may assert that a law or policy should be adopted, changed, or abandoned. As in the computer example, you may also explain to your reader that a situation or condition exists; rather than argue a viewpoint, you would use examples to illustrate your assertion about the essay's subject.

Specifically, the **subject** of Topic A is *the computer*. The **assertion** is that *it is a modern wonder that has improved our lives and that we rely on*. Now you quickly have created a workable thesis in a few moments.

> *The computer is a modern wonder of the world that has improved our lives and that we have come to rely on.*

Guidelines for Writing Thesis Statements

The following guidelines are not a formula for writing thesis statements, but rather are general strategies for making your thesis statement clearer and more effective.

1. State a *particular point of view* about the topic with both a *subject* and an *assertion.* The thesis should give the essay purpose and scope and thus provide the reader with a guide. If the thesis is vague, your essay may be undeveloped because you do not have an idea to assert or a point to explain. Weak thesis statements are often framed as facts, questions, or announcements:

   a. Avoid a fact statement as a thesis. While a fact statement may provide a subject, it generally does not include a point of view about the subject that provides the basis for an extended discussion. Example: *Recycling saved our community over $10,000 last year.* This fact statement provides a detail, *not* a point of view. Such a detail might be found within an essay, but it does not state a point of view.

   b. Avoid framing the thesis as a vague question. In many cases, rhetorical questions do not provide a clear point of view for an extended essay. Example: *How do people recycle?* This question neither asserts a point of view nor helpfully guides the reader to understand the essay's purpose and scope.

   c. Avoid the "announcer" topic sentence that merely states the topic you will discuss. Example: I *will discuss ways to recycle.* This sentence states the subject, but the scope of the essay is only suggested. Again, this statement does not assert a viewpoint that guides the essay's purpose. It merely "announces" that the writer will write about the topic.

2. Start with a workable thesis. You might revise your thesis as you begin writing and discover your own point of view.

3. If feasible and appropriate, perhaps state the thesis in multi-point form, expressing the scope of the essay. By stating the points in parallel form, you clearly lay out the essay's plan for the reader.
   Example: *To improve the environment, we can recycle our trash, elect politicians who see the environment as a priority, and support lobbying groups who work for environmental protection.*

4. Because of the exam time limit, place your thesis in the first paragraph to key the reader to the essay's main idea.

Creating a working outline

A good thesis gives structure to your essay and helps focus your thoughts. When forming your thesis, look at your prewriting strategy—clustering, questioning, or brainstorming. Then, decide quickly which two or three major areas you will discuss. Remember, you must limit *the scope* of the paper because of the time factor.

The **outline** lists those main areas or points as topics for each paragraph. Looking at the prewriting cluster on computers, you might choose several areas in which computers help us, e.g., in science and medicine, business, and education. You might also consider people's reliance on this "wonder" and include at least one paragraph about this reliance. A formal outline for this essay might look like the one below.

I.   Introduction and thesis
II. Computers used in science and medicine
II. Computers used in business
IV. Computers used in education
V. People's reliance on computers
VI. Conclusion

Under time pressure, however, you may use a shorter organizational plan, such as abbreviated key words in a list. For example:

1. intro: wonders of the computer -OR-   a. intro: wonders of computers—science
2. science   b. in the space industry
3. med   c. in medical technology
4. schools   d. conclusion
5. business
6. conclusion

Developing the essay

With a working thesis and outline, you can begin writing the essay. The essay should be in three main sections:

1) The **introduction** sets up the essay and leads to the thesis statement.
2) The **body paragraphs** are developed with concrete information leading from the **topic sentences**.
3) The **conclusion** ties the essay together.

Introduction

Put your thesis statement into a clear, coherent opening paragraph. One effective device is to use a funnel approach, in which you begin with a brief description of the broader issue and then move to a clearly focused, specific thesis statement.

Consider the following introductions to the essay on computers. The length of each is an obvious difference. Read each and consider the other differences.

> Does each introduce the subject generally?
> Does each lead to a stated thesis?
> Does each relate to the topic prompt?

Introduction 1: *Computers are used every day. They have many uses. Some people who use them are workers, teachers, and doctors.*

Analysis: This introduction does give the general topic, computers used every day, but it does not explain what those uses are. This introduction does not offer a point of view in a clearly stated thesis, nor does it convey the idea that computers are a modern wonder.

Introduction 2: *Computers are used just about everywhere these days. I do not think there is an office around that does not use computers, and we use them a lot in all kinds of jobs. Computers are great for making life easier and work better. I do not think we would get along without the computer.*

Analysis: This introduction gives the general topic about computers and mentions one area that uses computers. The thesis states that people could not get along without computers, but it does not state the specific areas the essay discusses. Note, too, the meaning is not helped by vague diction, such as *a lot* or *great.*

Introduction 3: *Each day we either use computers or see them being used around us. We wake to the sound of a digital alarm operated by a microchip. Our cars run by computerized machinery. We use computers to help us learn. We receive phone calls and letters transferred from computers across continents. Our astronauts walked on the moon, and returned safely, all because of computer technology. The computer is a wonderful electronic brain that we have come to rely on, and it has changed our world through advances in science, business, and education.*

Analysis: This introduction is the most thorough and fluent because it provides interest in the general topic and offers specific information about computers as a modern wonder. It also leads to a thesis that directs the reader to the scope of the discussion—advances in science, business, and education.

Topic Sentences

Just as the essay must have an overall focus reflected in the thesis statement, each paragraph must have a central idea reflected in the topic sentence. A good topic sentence also provides transition from the previous paragraph and relates to the essay's thesis. Good topic sentences, therefore, provide unity throughout the essay.

Consider the following potential topic sentences. Be sure that each provides transition and clearly states the subject of the paragraph.

Topic Sentence 1: *Computers are used in science.*

Analysis: This sentence simply states the topic—computers used in science. It does not relate to the thesis or provide transition from the introduction. The reader still does not know how computers are used.

Topic Sentence 2: *Now I will talk about computers used in science.*

Analysis: Like the faulty "announcer" thesis statement, this "announcer" topic sentence is vague and merely names the topic.

Topic Sentence 3: *First, computers used in science have improved our lives.*

Analysis: The transition word *First* helps link the introduction and this paragraph. It adds unity to the essay. It, however, does not give specifics about the improvement computers have made in our lives.

Topic Sentence 4: *First used in scientific research and spaceflights, computers are now used extensively in the diagnosis and treatment of disease.*

Analysis: This sentence is the most thorough and fluent. It provides specific areas that will be discussed in the paragraph and it offers more than an announcement of the topic. The writer gives concrete information about the content of the paragraph that will follow.

Summary Guidelines for Writing Topic Sentences
1. Specifically relate the topic to the thesis statement.
2. State clearly and concretely the subject of the paragraph.
3. Provide some transition from the previous paragraph.
4. Avoid topic sentences that are facts, questions, or announcers.

Supporting Details

If you have a good thesis and a good outline, you should be able to construct a complete essay. Your paragraphs should contain concrete, interesting information and supporting details to support your point of view. As often as possible, create images in your reader's mind. Fact statements also add weight to your opinions, especially when you are trying to convince the reader of your viewpoint. Because every good thesis has an assertion, you should offer specifics, facts, data, anecdotes, expert opinions, and other details to *show* or *prove* that assertion. While *you* know what you mean, your *reader* does not. On the exam, you must explain and develop ideas as fully as possible in the time allowed.

In the following paragraph, the sentences in **bold print** provide a skeleton of a paragraph on the benefits of recycling. The sentences in bold are generalizations that by themselves do not explain the need to recycle. The sentences in *italics* add details to SHOW the general points in bold. Notice how the supporting details help you understand the necessity for recycling.

While one day recycling may become mandatory in all states, right now, it is voluntary in many communities. *Those of us who participate in recycling are amazed by how much material is recycled.* **For many communities, the blue-box recycling program has had an immediate effect.** *By just recycling glass, aluminum cans, and plastic bottles, we have reduced the volume of disposable trash by one-third, thus extending the useful life of local landfills by over a decade. Imagine the difference if those dramatic results were achieved nationwide.* **The amount of reusable items we thoughtlessly dispose of is staggering.** *For example, Americans dispose of enough steel everyday to supply Detroit car manufacturers for three months. Additionally, we dispose of enough aluminum annually to rebuild the nation's air fleet. These statistics, available from the Environmental Protection Agency (EPA), should encourage all of us to watch what we throw away.* **Clearly, recycling in our homes and in our communities directly improves the environment.**

Notice how the author's supporting examples enhance the message of the paragraph and relate to the author's thesis noted above. If you only read the boldface sentences, you have a glimpse at the topic. This paragraph of illustration, however, is developed through numerous details creating specific images: *reduced the volume of disposable trash by one-third, extended the useful life of local landfills by over a decade, enough steel everyday to supply Detroit car manufacturers for three months, enough aluminum to rebuild the nation's air fleet.* If the writer had merely written a few general sentences, as those shown in bold print, you would not fully understand the vast amount of trash involved in recycling or the positive results of current recycling efforts.

End your essay with a brief straightforward **concluding paragraph** that ties together the essay's content and leaves the reader with a sense of its completion. The conclusion should reinforce the main points and offer some insight into the topic, provide a sense of unity for the essay by relating it to the thesis, and signal clear closure of the essay.

SAMPLE SUMMARY WRITING ASSIGNMENT

Exercise

In a written response for an audience of teachers, identify a grade/age level and subject area for which you are prepared to teach. Then use your knowledge of instruction and assessment to describe a "hands-on" activity or lesson that would help students to learn and apply new information.

Sample Response

For a second grade math lesson, I might teach students about fractions. While fractions are difficult to learn, students will quickly understand the concept of fractions if using manipulatives and hands-on activities.

First, I would draw a picture of a pie on the overhead. I would then start to draw lines all over the place—one piece would be very large, a few pieces would be quite small, and the last few would be regular pieces of pie. Students would recognize that the pieces are a variety of different sizes. I would then ask them to help me cut the pie so that each of my five guests would have a similarly sized slice.

The next step would be to put the students into small groups. I would give them cutouts of a pizza, and I would ask them to determine how many slices they would need to make sure everyone got one similarly sized slice, and then cut the pizza.

The final step of this "hands-on" lesson would be to have the groups show me what one-half a pizza would be. On each pizza, they would count their slices. This would continue until they understood that one-half or one-quarter could constitute a variety of numbers of slices depending upon how many slices were cut for each pizza.

This activity would help students learn the concept of fractions by giving them a practical, simple method of seeing fractions. They would understand that one pizza could have many different combinations of slices. Overall, this is a fun, practical, and useful way to teach the very difficult concept of fractions.

Evaluation

The NMTA uses a four-point holistic scoring guide to evaluate candidate responses. This response would receive a score of 4. This essay demonstrates a very good knowledge of "hands-on" activities in the teaching of math. It clearly shows how various concepts of instruction can be tailored for different learning styles and different instructional standards. The candidate shows a good working knowledge of the subarea by demonstrating the importance of carefully designing a lesson in order to meet students' learning needs. The lesson is very clear, and directions are provided step-by-step. No element of instruction is left out. Furthermore, the essay ends with a very good overview of how this lesson would meet students' learning needs, and it argues convincingly for using hands-on methods to teach this concept. Finally, the candidate chose a topic for which hands-on instruction would be very appropriate.

SAMPLE OPEN RESPONSE WRITING ASSIGNMENT

Student Learning: Standards-Driven or Project-Based?

In an age of accountability for student learning, many educators assume that sticking to standards and ensuring that each standard is covered explicitly is the safest and most prudent thing to do. However, many educators still believe that engaging students in academic and cross-curricular projects can cover standards, perhaps in a non-linear fashion. Those who believe that project-based instruction is more valuable suggest that students will enjoy their learning more and will still learn many important academic standards in the process. Those who believe that standards-driven learning is more valuable might argue that it is unfair to students not to cover every area on which they will be tested. They might also suggest that teaching standards in a linear fashion will provide greater clarity for students.

In a response written for an audience of teachers, use your knowledge of learners and the learning environment to analyze and discuss the issue of standards-driven and project-based teaching.

RESPONSE

There is no doubt that students must be prepared based on state standards. However, when analyzing state standards, it is important to realize that while standards may look like a bunch of unconnected skills, they really do build upon one another and there is quite a bit of information that overlaps. In my first year as a high school Language Arts teacher, I know that it is important to focus on both standards as well as engaging, meaningful projects. I do not believe that a teacher would have to choose between the two approaches, standards-driven and project-based.

When evaluating what to teach and how to teach it, it is important first to ensure that what is being taught can be defended by the standards. Teachers must make sure that students learn what is required, as students are tested on that material. They are also expected to know that material as they progress to the next grade level.

However, not all students will learn at the same pace and in the same way. Furthermore, if a teacher simply were to "cover" the standards, students would have little context for understanding the material, and it certainly would not be very exciting. Students need to feel that what they are learning is important beyond passing tests. For that reason, developing lessons, units, and projects that take students' varied learning styles into account and draw upon real-world examples and issues will make learning more fun, and it will ensure that all students learn. However, such lessons, units, and projects should also be based on standards so that students have interesting, enjoyable, and student-centered ways of learning the information they are required to know. This method seems to be a more logical approach that combines the positives of both positions.

An example of combining these two approaches, based on a secondary Language Arts classroom, is the teaching of literature. For example, a particular standard might call for students to understand imagery in literature. Another standard might call for students to learn about specific eras in American literature. Another might call for students to learn how to write an analysis of literary techniques. If I were to teach based on standards-driven principles, I would teach all these skills out of context. Yet, if I were to focus simply on a project-based method, I might not hit any of these issues. However, if I were to have students engage in a project that focused on each of these areas and gave them choice in the way they work toward the final project, while giving specialized assistance to those who need it, students will get the opportunity to learn these skills. They will more likely enjoy the process and learn at an appropriate pace.

Combining both approaches seems most logical. While many educators argue that standards-driven instruction is the only way to ensure that students are prepared for testing, doing so alone will provide little opportunity for students to learn in ways that are natural for them. On the other hand, while many educators are convinced that doing anything other than project-based instruction will be boring for students, not paying significant attention to standards will ensure that students are not prepared for the complex academic tasks they will be required to master.

EVALUATION

The assignment asked the candidate to analyze two claims, both at odds with each other. One side, suggesting that standards-driven instruction is more appropriate, seemingly goes against the other side, project-based instruction. Yet the candidate wrote an essay that effectively found the best of both methods. The essay demonstrates a deep knowledge of student learning, as well as contemporary issues of curriculum and instruction. It demonstrated knowledge of student engagement and standards-based instruction. Although the essay did not ask for the candidate to demonstrate the best of both models, its strength lies in the fact that it does indeed show how both methods have some limitations as well as some strengths. Putting both together with a good curricular example was effective. This essay demonstrates strong knowledge of Subarea 1 of the OPTE framework.

Sample Test: Reading

Read the passages and answer the questions that follow.

This writer has often been asked to tutor hospitalized children with cystic fibrosis. While undergoing all the precautionary measures to see these children (i.e. scrubbing thoroughly and donning sterilized protective gear for the children's protection), she has often wondered why their parents subject these children to the pressures of schooling and trying to catch up on what they have missed because of hospitalization, which is a normal part of cystic fibrosis patients' lives. These children undergo so many tortuous treatments a day that it seems cruel to expect them to learn as normal children do, especially with their life expectancies being as short as they are.

1. **What is meant by the word "precautionary" in the second sentence?**
    (Average Rigor) (Skill 1.2)

    A.   Careful
    B.   Protective
    C.   Medical
    X D.   Sterilizing

2. **What is the main idea of this passage?**
    (Average Rigor) (Skill 2.1)

    A.   There is a lot of preparation involved in visiting a patient with cystic fibrosis.
    B.   Children with cystic fibrosis are incapable of living normal lives.
    C.   Certain concessions should be made for children with cystic fibrosis.
    X D.   Children with cystic fibrosis die young.

3. **What is the author's purpose?**
    (Average Rigor) (Skill 3.1)

    A.   To inform
    B.   To entertain
    C.   To describe
    D.   To narrate

4. **What is the author's tone?**
    (Average Rigor) (Skill 3.2)

    A.   Sympathetic
    B.   Cruel
    C.   Disbelieving
    D.   Cheerful

5. **What kind of relationship is found within the last sentence that starts with "These children undergo..." and ends with "...as short as they are"?**
(Rigorous) (Skill 4.3)

    A.   Addition
    B.   Explanation
X C.   Generalization
    D.   Classification

6. **How is the author so familiar with the procedures used when visiting a child with cystic fibrosis?**
(Easy) (Skill 4.5)

    A.   She has read about it.
    B.   She works in a hospital.
    C.   She is the parent of one.
    D.   She often tutors them.

7. **Does the author present an argument that is valid or invalid concerning the schooling of children with cystic fibrosis?**
(Rigorous) (Skill 5.1)

X A.   Valid
    B.   Invalid

8. **The author states that it is "cruel" to expect children with cystic fibrosis to learn as "normal" children do. Is this a fact or an opinion?**
(Average Rigor) (Skill 5.5)

    A.   Fact
    B.   Opinion

9. **Is there evidence of bias in this paragraph?**
(Rigorous) (Skills 5.1 and 5.6)

    A.   Yes
    B.   No

10. **What type of organizational pattern is the author using?**
(Rigorous) (Skill 9.1)

    A.   Classification
    B.   Explanation
    C.   Comparison-and-contrast
    D.   Cause-and-effect

X

Disciplinary practices have been found to affect diverse areas of child development such as the acquisition of moral values, obedience to authority, and performance at school. Even though the dictionary has a specific definition of the word "discipline," it is still open to interpretation by people of different cultures.

There are four types of disciplinary styles: assertion of power, withdrawal of love, reasoning, and permissiveness. Assertion of power involves the use of force to discourage unwanted behavior. Withdrawal of love involves making the love of a parent conditional on a child's good behavior. Reasoning involves persuading the child to behave one way rather than another. Permissiveness involves allowing the child to do as he or she pleases and to face the consequences of his/her actions.

11. **What is the meaning of the word "diverse" in the first sentence?**
(Easy) (Skill 1.1)

    A.   Many
    B.   Related to children
    C.   Disciplinary
    D.   Moral

12. **What is the main idea of this passage?**
(Average Rigor) (Skill 2.2)

    A.   Different people have different ideas of what discipline is.
    B.   Permissiveness is the most widely used disciplinary style.
    C.   Most people agree on their definition of discipline.
    D.   There are four disciplinary styles.

13. **Which of the following elements will affect the audience's reaction to this selection?**
(Rigorous) (Skill 3.3)

    A.   Tone
    B.   Level of formality
    C.   Word choice
    D.   All of the above

14. **What is the author's tone?**
(Average Rigor) (Skill 3.4)

    A.   Disbelieving
    B.   Angry
    C.   Informative
    D.   Optimistic

15. **Name the four types of disciplinary styles.**
(Easy) (Skill 4.5)

    A.   Reasoning, power assertion, morality, and permissiveness

    B.   Morality, reasoning, permissiveness, and withdrawal of love

    C.   Withdrawal of love, permissiveness, assertion of power, and reasoning

    D.   Permissiveness, morality, reasoning, and power assertion

16. **From reading this passage, we can conclude that**
(Rigorous) (Skill 4.5)

    A.   The author is a teacher.

    B.   The author has many children.

    C.   The author has written a book about discipline.

    D.   The author has done much research on discipline.

17. **Is this passage biased?**
(Average Rigor) (Skills 5.1 and 5.6)

    A.   Yes

    B.   No

18. **The author states that "assertion of power involves the use of force to discourage unwanted behavior." Is this a fact or an opinion?**
(Average Rigor) (Skill 5.5)

    A.   Fact

    B.   Opinion

19. **What is the purpose of this selection?**
(Easy) (Skill 7.1)

    A.   To persuade

    B.   To describe

    C.   To inform

    D.   To tell a story

20. **What organizational structure is used in the first sentence of the second paragraph?**
(Average Rigor) (Skill 9.1)

    A.   Addition

    B.   Explanation

    C.   Definition

    D.   Simple listing

21. **What is the overall organizational pattern of this passage?**
(Rigorous) (Skill 9.1)

    A.   Generalization

    B.   Cause-and-effect

    C.   Addition

    D.   Summary

Select the best answer for the following multiple-choice questions.

22. **"The fall landscape was an artist's palette of rich colors" is an example of** *(Rigorous) (Skill 1.3)*

    A.   A hyperbole
    B.   A metaphor
    C.   Alliteration
    D.   An oxymoron

23. **The definition of onomatopoeia is** *(Rigorous) (Skill 1.3)*

    A.   A word or group of words that describes a sound, therefore suggesting the source of the sound
    B.   The arrangement of ideas in phrases, sentences, and paragraphs that balances one element with another of equal importance and similar wording
    C.   An exaggeration for effect or comic effect
    D.   The repetition of consonant sounds in two or more neighboring words or syllables

24. **The purpose of supporting details in a paragraph is to** *(Easy) (Skill 2.3)*

    A.   Summarize the main idea of the passage
    B.   Use facts, examples, anecdotes, etc. to show and/or expand on the main idea of the passage
    C.   Outline the passage
    D.   Provide unnecessary information about the passage

25. **Select the correct order of the following statements to provide the right sequence of events.** *(Easy) (Skill 4.1)*

    1.   Josh interviewed with a publishing company.
    2.   Josh mailed copies of his résumés to possible employers.
    3.   Josh completed a résumé course.
    4.   Josh began work as a junior copywriter.

    A.   1, 3, 4, 2
    B.   4, 2, 1, 3
    C.   3, 2, 1, 4
    D.   2, 1, 3, 4

26. **Which of the following statements shows a good example of a cause-effect relationship?**
(Average Rigor) (Skill 4.2)

   A. Janice got home late; therefore, she missed her TV program.
   B. Cities have grown very large, so factories have attracted many jobs.
   C. The weather outside was cold, and as a result, Sally opened a window.
   D. Jesse teased the cat because the cat growled.

27. **Ben is writing a short story about Jill, a girl who wants to be involved in her community one summer and has decided to raise money for a local animal shelter. Lacking adequate personal funds, Jill considers her options for raising money. What would be the optimal solution for Ben to use in his story, taking into account a good climax?**
(Rigorous) (Skill 4.4)

   A. Borrow money from friends
   B. Distribute a babysitting flyer to her neighbors and wait
   C. Get a job at a local department store
   D. Organize a car wash with friends to raise money for the shelter

Read the following passage and select the best answer.

The local homeless charity is planning to open a new soup kitchen located on Main Street. Their objective is to provide three well-rounded meals to as many as 75 homeless people each day. The kitchen will open at 7:00 in the morning for breakfast and will continue to serve food throughout the day until dinner is over at 6:30 p.m. The organizer of the charity is a woman. Local supermarkets have already agreed to supply food to the charity; however, they are still in need of volunteers to help run the food lines. In addition, further donations of money and food are still needed to supply the patrons adequately.

28. **Which sentence is irrelevant to the information in the passage?**
(Average Rigor) (Skill 5.2)

   A. Their objective is to provide three well-rounded meals to as many as 75 homeless people each day.
   B. The organizer of the charity is a woman.
   C. The local homeless charity is planning to open a new soup kitchen located on Main Street.
   D. Local supermarkets have already agreed to supply food to the charity; however, they are still in need of volunteers to help run the food lines.

Select the best answer to the following multiple-choice questions.

29. **The conclusion below is an example of a fallacy.**
    (Rigorous) (Skill 5.3)

    Premise 1: All horses are mammals.
    Premise 2: All whales are mammals.
    Conclusion: All horses are whales.

    A. True
    B. False

30. **Which of the following statements describes an analogy?**
    (Rigorous) (Skill 5.4)

    A. Analogies compare the likeness of things.
    B. Analogies support that if two things have something in common, then they likely have other things in common.
    C. Analogies do not result in false logic.
    D. All of the above.

Answer Key: Reading

1. B
2. C
3. C
4. A
5. B
6. D
7. B
8. B
9. A
10. B
11. A
12. A
13. D
14. C
15. C
16. D
17. B
18. A
19. C
20. D
21. C
22. B
23. A
24. B
25. C
26. A
27. D
28. B
29. A
30. C

Rigor Table: Reading

	Easy 20%	Average 40%	Rigorous 40%
Questions (30)	6, 11, 15, 19, 24, 25	1, 2, 3, 4, 8, 12, 14, 17, 18, 20, 26, 28	5, 7, 9, 10, 13, 16, 21, 22, 23, 27, 29, 30
TOTALS	6 (20.0%)	12 (40.0%)	12 (40.0%)

Rationales with Sample Questions: Reading

Read the following passage and answer the questions that follow.

This writer has often been asked to tutor hospitalized children with cystic fibrosis. While undergoing all the precautionary measures to see these children (i.e. scrubbing thoroughly and donning sterilized protective gear for the children's protection), she has often wondered why their parents subject these children to the pressures of schooling and trying to catch up on what they have missed because of hospitalization, which is a normal part of cystic fibrosis patients' lives. These children undergo so many tortuous treatments a day that it seems cruel to expect them to learn as normal children do, especially with their life expectancies being as short as they are.

1.　**What is meant by the word "precautionary" in the second sentence?**
   (Average Rigor) (Skill 1.2)

   A.　Careful
   B.　Protective
   C.　Medical
   D.　Sterilizing

Answer: B. Protective

The writer uses expressions such as "protective gear" and "children's protection" to emphasize this.

2.　**What is the main idea of this passage?**
   (Average Rigor) (Skill 2.1)

   A.　There is a lot of preparation involved in visiting a patient with cystic fibrosis.
   B.　Children with cystic fibrosis are incapable of living normal lives.
   C.　Certain concessions should be made for children with cystic fibrosis.
   D.　Children with cystic fibrosis die young.

Answer: C.　Certain concessions should be made for children with cystic fibrosis.

The author states that she wonders, "why parents subject these children to the pressures of schooling" and that "it seems cruel to expect them to learn as normal children do." In making these statements, she appears to be expressing the belief that these children should not have to do what "normal" children do. They have enough to deal with—their illness itself.

3.   **What is the author's purpose?**
        (Average Rigor) (Skill 3.1)

        A.   To inform
        B.   To entertain
        C.   To describe
        D.   To narrate

Answer: C. To describe

The author is simply describing her experience in working with children with cystic fibrosis.

4.   **What is the author's tone?** *(Average Rigor) (Skill 3.2)*

        A.   Sympathetic
        B.   Cruel
        C.   Disbelieving
        D.   Cheerful

Answer: A. Sympathetic

The author states, "it seems cruel to expect them to learn as normal children do," thereby indicating that she feels sorry for them.

5.   **What kind of relationship is found within the last sentence which starts with "These children undergo..." and ends with "...as short as they are"?**
        (Rigorous) (Skill 4.3)

        A.   Addition
        B.   Explanation
        C.   Generalization
        D.   Classification

Answer: B. Explanation

In mentioning that their life expectancies are short, she is explaining by giving one reason why it is cruel to expect them to learn as normal children do.

6. How is the author so familiar with the procedures used when visiting a child with cystic fibrosis?
(Easy) (Skill 4.5)

    A.   She has read about it.
    B.   She works in a hospital.
    C.   She is the parent of one.
    D.   She often tutors them.

Answer: D. She often tutors them.

The writer states this fact in the opening sentence.

7. Does the author present an argument that is valid or invalid concerning the schooling of children with cystic fibrosis?
(Rigorous) (Skill 5.1)

    A.   Valid
    B.   Invalid

Answer: B. Valid

Even though the writer's argument makes good sense to most readers, it shows bias and lacks real evidence.

8. The author states that it is "cruel" to expect children with cystic fibrosis to learn as "normal" children do. Is this a fact or an opinion?
(Average Rigor) (Skill 5.5)

    A.   Fact
    B.   Opinion

Answer: B. Opinion

The fact that she states that it "seems" cruel indicates there is no evidence to support this belief.

9. **Is there evidence of bias in this paragraph?**
(Rigorous) (Skills 5.1 and 5.6)

A. Yes
B. No

Answer: A. Yes

The writer clearly feels sorry for these children and gears her writing in that direction.

10. **What type of organizational pattern is the author using?**
(Rigorous) (Skill 9.1)

A. Classification
B. Explanation
C. Comparison-and-contrast
D. Cause-and-effect

Answer: B. Explanation

The author mentions tutoring children with cystic fibrosis in her opening sentence and goes on to "explain" some of the issues that are involved with her job.

Read the following passage and answer the questions that follow.

Disciplinary practices have been found to affect diverse areas of child development such as the acquisition of moral values, obedience to authority, and performance at school. Even though the dictionary has a specific definition of the word "discipline," it is still open to interpretation by people of different cultures.

There are four types of disciplinary styles: assertion of power, withdrawal of love, reasoning, and permissiveness. Assertion of power involves the use of force to discourage unwanted behavior. Withdrawal of love involves making the love of a parent conditional on a child's good behavior. Reasoning involves persuading the child to behave one way rather than another. Permissiveness involves allowing the child to do as he or she pleases and to face the consequences of his/her actions.

11. **What is the meaning of the word "diverse" in the first sentence?**
   (Easy) (Skill 1.1)

   A.   Many
   B.   Related to children
   C.   Disciplinary
   D.   Moral

Answer: A. Many

Any of the other choices would be redundant in this sentence.

12. **What is the main idea of this passage?**
   (Average Rigor) (Skill 2.2)

   A.   Different people have different ideas of what discipline is.
   B.   Permissiveness is the most widely used disciplinary style.
   C.   Most people agree on their definition of discipline.
   D.   There are four disciplinary styles.

Answer: A. Different people have different ideas of what discipline is.

Choice C is not true; the opposite is stated in the passage. Choice B could be true, but we have no evidence of this. Choice D is just one of the many facts listed in the passage.

13. **Which of the following elements will affect the audience's reaction to this selection?**
   (Rigorous) (Skill 3.3)

   A.   Tone
   B.   Level of formality
   C.   Word choice
   D.   All of the above

Answer: D. All of the above

Tone, level of formality in the writing, and word choice are all elements of writing that affect how the audience reacts to a written piece.

14. **What is the author's tone?** *(Average Rigor) (Skill 3.4)*

   A.   Disbelieving
   B.   Angry
   C.   Informative
   D.   Optimistic

Answer: C. Informative

The author appears simply to be stating the facts.

15. **Name the four types of disciplinary styles.**
   (Easy) (Skill 4.5)

   A.   Reasoning, power assertion, morality, and permissiveness
   B.   Morality, reasoning, permissiveness, and withdrawal of love
   C.   Withdrawal of love, permissiveness, assertion of power, and reasoning
   D.   Permissiveness, morality, reasoning, and power assertion

Answer: C. Withdrawal of love, permissiveness, assertion of power, and reasoning

This is directly stated in the second paragraph.

16. **From reading this passage, we can conclude that**
   (Rigorous) (Skill 4.5)

   A.   The author is a teacher.
   B.   The author has many children.
   C.   The author has written a book about discipline.
   D.   The author has done much research on discipline.

Answer: D. The author has done much research on discipline.

Given all the facts mentioned in the passage, this is the only inference one can make.

17.   Is this passage biased? *(Average Rigor) (Skills 5.1 and 5.6)*

    A.   Yes
    B.   No

Answer: B. No

If the reader were so inclined, he could research discipline and find this information.

18.   **The author states "assertion of power involves the use of force to discourage unwanted behavior." Is this a fact or an opinion?** *(Average Rigor) (Skill 5.5)*

    A.   Fact
    B.   Opinion

Answer: A. Fact

The author appears to have done extensive research on this subject.

19.   **What is the purpose of this selection?** *(Easy) (Skill 7.1)*

    A.   To persuade
    B.   To describe
    C.   To inform
    D.   To tell a story

Answer: C. To inform

The purpose of this piece is to inform the reader of four basic disciplinary styles.

20.   **What organizational structure is used in the first sentence of the second paragraph?** *(Average Rigor) (Skill 9.1)*

    A.   Addition
    B.   Explanation
    C.   Definition
    D.   Simple listing

Answer: D. Simple listing

The author simply states the types of disciplinary styles.

21. **What is the overall organizational pattern of this passage?**
    (Rigorous) (Skill 9.1)

    A. Generalization
    B. Cause-and-effect
    C. Addition
    D. Summary

Answer: C. Addition

The author has taken a subject, in this case discipline, and developed it point by point.

Select the best answer for the following multiple-choice questions.

22. **"The fall landscape was an artist's palette of rich colors" is an example of**
    (Rigorous) (Skill 1.3)

    A. A hyperbole
    B. A metaphor
    C. Alliteration
    D. An oxymoron

Answer: B. A metaphor

A metaphor makes a comparison between two unrelated items without using the words "like" or "as."

23. **The definition of onomatopoeia is**
    (Rigorous) (Skill 1.3)

    A. A word or group of words that describes a sound, therefore suggesting the source of the sound
    B. The arrangement of ideas in phrases, sentences, and paragraphs that balance one element with another of equal importance and similar wording
    C. An exaggeration for effect or comic effect
    D. The repetition of consonant sounds in two or more neighboring words or syllables

Answer: A. A word or group of words that describes a sound, therefore suggesting the source of the sound

Choice A is the correct definition. Choice B defines parallelism; Choice C defines a hyperbole; and Choice D defines alliteration.

24.   **The purpose of supporting details in a paragraph is to**
        (Easy) (Skill 2.3)

        A.   Summarize the main idea of the passage
        B.   Use facts, examples, anecdotes, etc. to show and/or expand on the
                main idea of the passage
        C.   Outline the passage
        D.   Provide unnecessary information about the passage

Answer: B. Use facts, examples, anecdotes, etc. to show and/or expand
**   on the main idea of the passage**

Supporting details are used to expand on the statements in a paragraph. They
assist the author in showing support for the main idea of the writing.

25.   **Select the correct order of the following statements to provide the**
        right sequence of events.
        (Easy) (Skill 4.1)

        1.   Josh interviewed with a publishing company.
        2.   Josh mailed copies of his resumes to possible employers.
        3.   Josh completed a resume course.
        4.   Josh began work as a junior copywriter.

        A.   1, 3, 4, 2
        B.   4, 2, 1, 3
        C.   3, 2, 1, 4
        D.   2, 1, 3, 4

Answer: C. 3, 2, 1, 4

This is the only proper sequence of events for these actions.

26. **Which of the following statements shows a good example of a cause-effect relationship?**
(Average Rigor) (Skill 4.2)

   A.   Janice got home late; therefore, she missed her TV program.
   B.   Cities have grown very large, so factories have attracted many jobs.
   C.   The weather outside was cold, and as a result, Sally opened a window.
   D.   Jesse teased the cat because the cat growled.

Answer: A. Janice got home late; therefore, she missed her TV program.

Choice A shows the proper cause-effect relationship. Choices B, C, and D all have the effect listed first and then the cause, so the relationship is not appropriate.

27. **Ben is writing a short story about Jill, a girl who wants to be involved in her community one summer and has decided to raise money for a local animal shelter. Lacking adequate personal funds, Jill considers her options for raising money. What would be the optimal solution for Ben to use in his story, taking into account a good climax?**
(Rigorous) (Skill 4.4)

   A.   Borrow money from friends
   B.   Distribute a babysitting flyer to her neighbors and wait
   C.   Get a job at a local department store
   D.   Organize a car wash with friends to raise money for the shelter

Answer: D. Organize a car wash with friends to raise money for the shelter.

Choices A, B, and C do not attempt to include the community, nor do they show much action for Jill's character. Choice D is suited for a summer activity and has the most potential for a fun and quick way to earn money.

Read the following passage and select the best answer.

The local homeless charity is planning to open a new soup kitchen located on Main Street. Their objective is to provide three well-rounded meals to as many as 75 homeless people each day. The kitchen will open at 7:00 in the morning for breakfast and will continue to serve food throughout the day until dinner is over at 6:30 p.m. The organizer of the charity is a woman. Local supermarkets have already agreed to supply food to the charity; however, they are still in need of volunteers to help run the food lines. In addition, further donations of money and food are still needed to supply the patrons adequately.

28. **Which sentence is irrelevant to the information in the passage?**
    (Average Rigor) (Skill 5.2)

    A. Their objective is to provide three well-rounded meals to as many as 75 homeless people each day.
    B. The organizer of the charity is a woman.
    C. The local homeless charity is planning to open a new soup kitchen located on Main Street.
    D. Local supermarkets have already agreed to supply food to the charity; however, they are still in need of volunteers to help run the food lines.

Answer: B. The organizer of the charity is a woman.

Choices A, C, and D are all important pieces of information that relate to the opening of the homeless shelter. Choice B is an interesting fact to know, but without more detail (such as her name), the fact that the organizer is a woman is irrelevant.

Select the best answer to the following multiple-choice questions.

29. **The conclusion below is an example of a fallacy.**
    (Rigorous) (Skill 5.3)

    Premise 1: All horses are mammals.
    Premise 2: All whales are mammals.
    Conclusion: All horses are whales.

    A. True
    B. False

Answer: A. True

This conclusion is a fallacy, or error in reasoning, as the conclusion is an incorrect one based on insufficient information.

30. **Which of the following statements describes an analogy?**
(Rigorous) (Skill 5.4)

   A.   Analogies compare the likeness of things.
   B.   Analogies support that if two things have something in common, they likely have other things in common.
   C.   Analogies do not result in false logic.
   D.   All of the above

Answer: C. Analogies do not result in false logic.

Analogies can result in false logic and arguments. An example in Skill 5.4 stated

For example, peaches and plums are both fruits that have chemicals good for people to eat. Both peaches and plums are circular in shape; thus, it could be argued by analogy that "because" something is circular in shape, it is fruit and something good for people to eat. However, this analogical deduction is not logical (for example, a baseball is circular in shape but hardly good to eat).

Sample Test: Writing

DIRECTIONS: *Select the best multiple-choice answer for the following questions.*

1. **Mapping the text is an important reading strategy that helps to**
    (Rigorous) (Skill 6.1)

    A. Connect concepts and ideas in the reading by using colors, lines, pictures, and words to comprehend the meaning of the text
    B. Show where the text takes place
    C. Connect the reading to other related subjects and texts
    D. None of the above

2. **When creating an outline, it is important to teach students**
    (Rigorous) (Skill 6.1)

    A. To write neatly
    B. To include as much information as possible
    C. To include somewhat accurate information
    D. How headings and subheadings are used to point out the main ideas in the text

3. **When providing students with directions, whether oral or written, it is best to review the directions with the students. Which of the following answers is considered good practice when reviewing directions?**
    (Rigorous) (Skill 6.2)

    A. Rewording the directions for clarity
    B. Have students ask questions about and restate the directions before starting
    C. Use varying voice intonations as well as formats for the directions (i.e. present them orally, written on the page and/or on the board, etc.)
    D. All of the above

4. **When aiding a student who is having difficulty with directions, a good strategy for the student to try is to**
    (Rigorous) (Skill 6.2)

    A. Read the directions only once
    B. Actively read the directions thoroughly and multiple times if needed
    C. Scan the directions
    D. Avoid having the students rephrase the directions to the teacher

5. The following chart shows the yearly average number of international tourists visiting Palm Beach for 1990–1994. How many more tourists that are international visited Palm Beach in 1994 than in 1991? *(Easy) (Skill 6.3)*

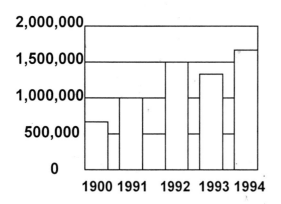

A. 100,000
B. 600,000
C. 1,600,000
D. 8,000,000

6. Which statement is true about George's budget? *(Easy) (Skill 6.3)*

A. George spends the greatest portion of his income on food.
B. George spends twice as much on utilities as he does on his mortgage.
C. George spends twice as much on utilities as he does on food.
D. George spends the same amount on food and utilities as he does on mortgage.

DIRECTIONS: *Read the following passage and answer the questions that follow.*

Rainforests are an endangered habitat on our planet. Found primarily around the Equator, rainforests are categorized as climates with dense humidity, warm temperatures, and high amounts of rainfall—over 80 inches each year.

Extremely important to the Earth's ecology, rainforests provide homes to millions of plants, animals, and food resources. The plants of the rainforest generate rich oxygen for much of the Earth, and if their destruction persists, the damage to the rainforests will cause a dangerous threat to the planet's ecological balance. If the trees and plants fail to grow, the planet is deprived of many of the natural food resources of the rainforest, including cocoa, coffee, sugar cane, and many varieties of nuts, fruits and spices.

Rainforests also recycle air and clean water. The trees capture and remove a large amount of the carbon dioxide in the air. This decreases the temperature of the overall planet, therefore affecting the greenhouse effect, which traps heat in the Earth's atmosphere.

Land seizure is one of the leading threats to the rainforest. If this destruction continues, it will surely result in further critical environmental issues.

7. **Which statement best summarizes this passage? (Rigorous) (Skill 6.3)**

    A. Rainforests recycle water sources and provide many types of food resources as well.
    B. The Earth consists of many rainforests around its Equator, and they are an important habitat.
    C. Threats to the rainforest, including land seizure, are very dangerous to the rainforests' existence.
    D. Rainforests are currently an endangered habitat and the continued threats to them may be detrimental to the Earth's ecosystems.

8. **Which fact(s) from the passage would most likely not be included in a summary about this topic? (Rigorous) (Skill 6.3)**

    A. The rainforest traps the heat in the Earth's atmosphere.
    B. The rainforests are an endangered habitat.
    C. There are dangerous threats to the rainforest.
    D. The rainforests play an important role in the balance of the Earth's ecosystems.

DIRECTIONS: *Select the best answer for the following multiple-choice questions.*

9. **Select the statement below that is true about journalistic writing.**
   (Average Rigor) (Skill 7.1)

   A. Journalism should contain biased statements.
   B. Journalism should convey information about a person, place, or event in a factual and objective manner.
   C. Using newspapers in the classroom is not a good tool for teaching.
   D. All of the above

10. **Which pairing below is the best example of matching an appropriate audience for the type of writing?**
    (Average Rigor) (Skill 7.2)

    A. Creative narrative story to a younger sibling
    B. Friendly letter with slang to a teacher
    C. History essay to a local politician
    D. Business letter to a friend

11. **When determining your tone and audience for a piece of writing, which of the following statements is likely to be the least considered?**
    (Rigorous) (Skill 7.2)

    A. What emotional qualities do I want to transmit in this writing?
    B. What choice of language is best suited for my audience?
    C. How lengthy should I make this piece?
    D. What does the person already know about this topic?

DIRECTIONS: *Choose the underlined word or phrase that is unnecessary within the context of the passage.*

12. **Considered by many to be one of the worst terrorist incidents on American soil was the bombing of the Oklahoma City Federal Building which will be remembered for years to come.**
    (Average Rigor) (Skill 8.1)

    A. Considered by many to be
    B. terrorist
    C. on American soil
    D. for years to come

13. The <u>flu</u> epidemic struck
<u>most of</u> the <u>respected</u>
faculty and students of
the Woolbright School ,
forcing the Boynton Beach
school superintendent to
close it down <u>for two
weeks.</u>
(Average Rigor) (Skill 8.1)

A. flu
B. most of
C. respected
D. for two weeks

14. The <u>expanding</u> number of
television channels has
<u>prompted</u> cable operators
to raise their prices, <u>even
though</u> many consumers
do not want to pay a
higher <u>increased</u> amount
for their service.
(Easy) (Skill 8.1)

A. expanding
B. prompted
C. even though
D. increased

DIRECTIONS: *Select the best
answer for the following multiple-
choice questions.*

15. Which of the following should
not be included in the
opening paragraph of
an informative essay?
(Average Rigor) (Skill 8.3)

A. Thesis sentence
B. Details and examples
supporting the main idea
C. A broad general introduction
to the topic
D. A style and tone that grab
the reader's attention

16. Which of the following should
not be included in the
opening paragraph of a
creative writing piece?
(Average Rigor) (Skill 8.3)

A. Dialogue
B. Thesis statement
C. Introduction of characters
and setting
D. A style and tone that grab
the reader's attention

DIRECTIONS: *For the underlined sentence(s), choose the option that expresses the meaning with the most fluency and the clearest logic within the context. If the underlined sentence should not be changed, choose Option A, which shows no change.*

17. **Selecting members of a President's cabinet can often be an aggravating process. Either there are too many or too few qualified candidates for a certain position, and then they have to be confirmed by the Senate, where there is the possibility of rejection.**
(Rigorous) (Skill 9.2)

A. Either there are too many or too few qualified candidates for a certain position, and then they have to be confirmed by the Senate, where there is the possibility of rejection.

B. Qualified candidates for certain positions face the possibility of rejection, when they have to be confirmed by the Senate.

C. The Senate has to confirm qualified candidates, who face the possibility of rejection.

D. Because the Senate has to confirm qualified candidates, they face the possibility of rejection.

18. **Treating patients for drug and/or alcohol abuse is a sometimes difficult process. Even though there are a number of different methods for helping the patient overcome a dependency, there is no way of knowing which is best in the long run.**
(Rigorous) (Skill 9.2)

A. Even though there are a number of different methods for helping the patient overcome a dependency, there is no way of knowing which is best in the long run.

B. Even though different methods can help a patient overcome a dependency, there is no way to know which is best in the long run.

C. Even though there is no way to know which way is best in the long run, patients can overcome their dependencies when they are helped.

D. There is no way to know which method will help the patient overcome a dependency in the long run, even though there are many different ones.

19. **Many factors account for the decline in quality of public education.** <u>**Overcrowding, budget cutbacks, and societal deterioration, which have greatly affected student learning.**</u>
    (Rigorous) (Skill 9.2)

    A. Overcrowding, budget cutbacks, and societal deterioration, which have greatly affected student learning.

    B. Student learning has been greatly affected by overcrowding, budget cutbacks, and societal deterioration.

    C. Due to overcrowding, budget cutbacks, and societal deterioration, student learning has been greatly affected.

    D. Overcrowding, budget cutbacks, and societal deterioration have affected students learning greatly.

DIRECTIONS: *Choose the sentence that logically and correctly expresses the comparison. (Easy) (Skill 9.2)*

20. A. The Empire State Building in New York is taller than buildings in the city.

    B. The Empire State Building in New York is taller than any other building in the city.

    C. The Empire State Building in New York is tallest than other buildings in the city.

DIRECTIONS: *In the sample paragraph below, choose the underlined transition that is not used effectively.*

21. **Autumn is my favorite time of year.** <u>**First**</u>**, the crisp, clean air is refreshing after the humid days of summer.** <u>**In addition**</u>**, I love the cinnamon smells in the kitchen of apple pies and cider. I** <u>**also**</u> **enjoy the beautiful colors of the trees in autumn, too.** <u>**In contrast,**</u> **October brings my favorite holiday, Halloween, when everyone dresses up!** <u>**In sum**</u>**, the holidays, smells, and sights make autumn the best time of year.**
    (Average Rigor) (Skill 9.3)

    A. First
    B. In addition
    C. In contrast
    D. In sum

DIRECTIONS: *Select the best answer for the following multiple-choice questions.*

22. Transitional words and phrases help to
(Average Rigor) (Skill 9.3)

A. Add structure to a text
B. Signal relationships between ideas in a text
C. Enhance the flow of writing
D. All of the above

23. Which of the following is a complex sentence?
(Rigorous) (Skill 10.2)

A. Anna and Margaret read fifty-four books during summer vacation.
B. The youngest boy on the team had the best earned run average, which mystifies the coaching staff.
C. Earl decided to attend Princeton; his twin brother Roy, who aced the ASVAB test, will be going to Annapolis.
D. "Easy come, easy go," Marcia moaned.

DIRECTIONS: *Choose the most effective word within the context of the sentence.*

24. Many of the clubs in Boca Raton are noted for their _____ elegance.
(Average Rigor) (Skill 10.5)

A. vulgar
B. tasteful
C. ordinary

25. When a student is expelled from school, the parents are usually _____ in advance.
(Average Rigor) (Skill 10.5)

A. rewarded
B. congratulated
C. notified

26. Before appearing in court, the witness was _____ the papers requiring her to show up.
(Average Rigor) (Skill 10.5)

A. condemned
B. served
C. criticized

DIRECTIONS: *The passage below contains many errors. Read the passage. Then answer each test item by choosing the option that corrects an error in the underlined portion(s). No more than one underlined error will appear in each item. If no error exists, choose "No change is necessary."*

Climbing to the top of Mount Everest is an adventure. One which everyone—whether physically fit or not—seems eager to try. The trail stretches for miles, the cold temperatures are usually frigid and brutal.

Climbers must endure severel barriers on the way, including other hikers, steep jagged rocks, and lots of snow. Plus, climbers often find the most grueling part of the trip is their climb back down, just when they are feeling greatly exhausted. Climbers who take precautions are likely to find the ascent less arduous than the unprepared. By donning heavy flannel shirts, gloves, and hats, climbers prevented hypothermia, as well as simple frostbite. A pair of rugged boots is also one of the necesities. If climbers are to avoid becoming dehydrated, there is beverages available for them to transport as well.

Once climbers are completely ready to begin their lengthy journey, they can comfortable enjoy the wonderful scenery. Wide rock formations dazzle the observers eyes with shades of gray and white, while the peak forms a triangle that seems to touch the sky. Each of the climbers are reminded of the splendor and magnifisence of Gods great Earth.

27. **Climbers must endure severel barriers on the way, including other hikers, steep jagged rocks, and lots of snow.**
(Easy) (Skill 8:2)

A. several
B. on the way: including
C. hikers'
D. No change is necessary

28. **A pair of rugged boots is also one of the necesities.**
(Rigorous) (Skill 8.2)

A. are
B. also, one
C. necessities
D. No change is necessary

29. **Plus, climbers often find the most grueling part of the trip is their climb back down, just when they are feeling greatly exhausted.**
(Average Rigor) (Skill 10.1)

A. his
B. down; just
C. were
D. No change is necessary

30. **Climbing to the top of Mount Everest is an adventure. One which everyone—whether physically fit or not—seems eager to try.**
(Rigorous) (Skill 10.2)

A. adventure, one
B. people, whether
C. seem
D. No change is necessary

31. <u>Climbers who</u> take precautions are likely to find the ascent <u>less difficult than</u> the unprepared.
(Average Rigor) (Skill 10.2)

A. Climbers, who
B. least difficult
C. then
D. No change is necessary

32. If climbers are to avoid <u>becoming</u> dehydrated, there <u>is</u> beverages available for <u>them</u> to transport as well.
(Easy) (Skill 10.3)

A. becomming
B. are
C. him
D. No change is necessary

33. Each of the climbers <u>are</u> reminded of the splendor and <u>magnifisence</u> of <u>God's</u> great Earth.
(Rigorous) (Skill 10.3)

A. is
B. magnifisence
C. Gods
D. No change is necessary

34. By donning heavy flannel shirts, boots, and <u>hats, climbers</u> <u>prevented</u> hypothermia, as well as simple frostbite.
(Average Rigor) (Skill 10.4)

A. hats climbers
B. can prevent
C. hypothermia;
D. No change is necessary

35. Once climbers are completely prepared for <u>their</u> lengthy <u>journey, they</u> can <u>comfortable</u> enjoy the wonderful scenery.
(Easy) (Skill 11.3)

A. they're
B. journey; they
C. comfortably
D. No change is necessary

36. Wide rock formations dazzle the <u>observers eyes</u> with shades of gray and <u>white, while</u> the peak <u>forms</u> a triangle that seems to touch the sky.
(Rigorous) (Skill 11.3)

A. observers' eyes
B. white; while
C. formed
D. No change is necessary

37. The <u>trail</u> stretches for <u>miles,</u> the cold temperatures are <u>usually</u> frigid and brutal.
(Rigorous) (Skill 11.4)

A. trails
B. miles;
C. usual
D. No change is necessary

DIRECTIONS: *The passage below contains several errors. Read the passage. Then answer each test item by choosing the option that corrects an error in the underlined portion(s). No more than one underlined error will appear in each item. If no error exists, choose "No change is necessary."*

Every job places different kinds of demands on their employees. For example, whereas such jobs as accounting and bookkeeping require mathematical ability; graphic design requires creative/artistic ability.

Doing good at one job does not usually guarantee success at another. However, one of the elements crucial to all jobs are especially notable: the chance to accomplish a goal.

The accomplishment of the employees varies according to the job. In many jobs the employees become accustom to the accomplishment provided by the work they do every day.

In medicine, for example, every doctor tests him self by treating badly injured or critically ill people. In the operating room, a team of Surgeons, is responsible for operating on many of these patients. In addition to the feeling of accomplishment that the workers achieve, some jobs also give a sense of identity to the employees'. Profesions like law, education, and sales offer huge financial and emotional rewards. Politicians are public servants: who work for the federal and state governments. President bush is basically employed by the American people to make laws and run the country.

Finally; the contributions that employees make to their companies and to the world cannot be taken for granted. Through their work, employees are performing a service for their employers and are contributing something to the world.

38. <u>However,</u> one of the elements crucial to all jobs <u>are</u> especially <u>notable:</u> the accomplishment of a goal.
(Average Rigor) (Skill 10.3)

   A. However
   B. is
   C. notable;
   D. No change is necessary

39. The <u>accomplishment</u> of the <u>employees</u> <u>varies</u> according to the job.
(Rigorous) (Skill 10.3)

   A. accomplishment,
   B. employee's
   C. vary
   D. No change is necessary

40. In many jobs the employees <u>become</u> <u>accustom</u> to the accomplishment <u>provided</u> by the work they do every day.
(Average Rigor) (Skill 11.1)

   A. became
   B. accustomed
   C. provides
   D. No change is necessary

41. Every job <u>places</u> different kinds of demands on <u>their</u> <u>employees</u>.
(Rigorous) (Skill 11.2)

A. place
B. its
C. employes
D. No change is necessary

42. In medicine, for example, every doctor <u>tests</u> <u>him self</u> by treating badly injured and critically ill people.
(Average Rigor) (Skill 11.2)

A. test
B. himself
C. critical
D. No change is necessary

43. Doing <u>good</u> at one job does not <u>usually</u> guarantee <u>success</u> at another.
(Rigorous) (Skill 11.3)

A. well
B. usualy
C. succeeding
D. No change is necessary

44. In addition to the feeling of accomplishment that the workers <u>achieve</u>, some jobs also <u>give</u> a sense of self-identity to the <u>employees'</u>.
(Average Rigor) (Skill 11.3)

A. acheive
B. gave
C. employees
D. No change is necessary

45. <u>For example</u>, <u>whereas</u> such jobs as accounting and bookkeeping require mathematical <u>ability;</u> graphic design requires creative/artistic ability.
(Average Rigor) (Skill 11.4)

A. For example
B. whereas,
C. ability,
D. No change is necessary

46. In the <u>operating room</u>, a team of <u>Surgeons, is</u> responsible for operating on many of <u>these</u> patients.
(Easy) (Skill 11.4)

A. operating room:
B. surgeons is
C. those
D. No change is necessary

47. <u>Profesions</u> like law, <u>education,</u> and sales <u>offer</u> huge financial and emotional rewards.
(Rigorous) (Skill 11.4)

A. Professions
B. education;
C. offered
D. No change is necessary

48. Politicians <u>are</u> public <u>servants: who work</u> for the federal and state governments.
(Easy) (Skill 11.4)

A. were
B. servants who
C. worked
D. No change is necessary

49. President <u>bush</u> is basically employed <u>by</u> the American people to <u>make</u> laws and run the country.
(Easy) (Skill 11.4)

   A. Bush
   B. to
   C. made
   D. No change is necessary

50. <u>Finally;</u> the contributions that employees make to <u>their</u> companies and to the world cannot be <u>taken</u> for granted.
(Average Rigor) (Skill 11.4)

   A. Finally,
   B. their
   C. took
   D. No change is necessary

Answer Key: Writing

1.	A		26.	B
2.	D		27.	A
3.	D		28.	C
4.	B		29.	D
5.	B		30.	A
6.	C		31.	D
7.	D		32.	B
8.	A		33.	A
9.	B		34.	B
10.	A		35.	C
11.	C		36.	A
12.	A		37.	B
13.	C		38.	B
14.	D		39.	C
15.	B		40.	B
16.	B		41.	B
17.	C		42.	B
18.	B		43.	A
19.	B		44.	C
20.	B		45.	C
21.	C		46.	B
22.	D		47.	A
23.	B		48.	B
24.	B		49.	A
25.	C		50.	A

Rigor Table: Writing

	Easy 20%	Average 40%	Rigorous 40%
Questions (50)	5, 6, 14, 20, 27, 32, 35, 46, 48, 49	9, 10, 12, 13, 15, 16, 21, 22, 24, 25, 26, 29, 31, 34, 38, 40, 42, 44, 45, 50	1, 2, 3, 4, 7, 8, 11, 17, 18, 19, 23, 28, 30, 33, 36, 37, 39, 41, 43, 47
TOTALS	10 (20.0%)	20 (40.0%)	20 (40.0%)

Rationales with Sample Questions: Writing

Select the best multiple-choice answer for the following questions.

1. **Mapping the text is an important reading strategy that helps to (Rigorous) (Skill 6.1)**

    A. Connect concepts and ideas in the reading by using colors, lines, pictures, and words to comprehend the meaning of the text
    B. Show where the text takes place
    C. Connect the reading to other related subjects and texts
    D. None of the above

Answer: A.   Connect concepts and ideas in the reading by using colors, lines, pictures, and words to comprehend the meaning of the text

Mapping allows the reader to maneuver through the meaning of a text by connecting concepts and ideas in the reading by using colors, lines, pictures, and words.

2. **When creating an outline, it is important to teach students (Rigorous) (Skill 6.1)**

    A. To write neatly
    B. To include as much information as possible
    C. To include somewhat accurate information
    D. How headings and subheadings are used to point out the main ideas in the text

Answer: D.   How headings and subheadings are used to point out the main ideas in the text

In outlines, concise and accurate headings and subheadings are very important to the outline's effectiveness as a study tool. Students must learn to include the most important information in these headings so they can use it to recall what was most important about what was learned.

3. **When providing students with directions, whether oral or written, it is best to review the directions with the students. Which of the following answers is considered good practice when reviewing directions?** *(Rigorous) (Skill 6.2)*

   A. Rewording the directions for clarity
   B. Have students ask questions about and restate the directions the directions before starting.
   C. Use varying voice intonations as well as formats for the directions (i.e. present them orally, written on the page and/or on the board, etc.).
   D. All of the above

Answer: D. All of the above

When presenting students with directions for a test or assignment, all of the answers listed are considered good practice for the teacher to utilize with his/her students. Rewording directions, having students ask questions and/or restate the directions back to you, and varying the way the directions are presented are all good ways to ensure the students clearly understand what to do.

4. **When aiding a student who is having difficulty with directions, a good strategy for the student to try is to** *(Rigorous) (Skill 6.2)*

   A. Read the directions only once
   B. Actively read the directions thoroughly and multiple times if needed
   C. Scan the directions
   D. Avoid having the students rephrase the directions to the teacher

Answer: B. Actively read the directions thoroughly and multiple times if needed

Encouraging students to read actively, rather than just scan, the directions is a good way to help a student who is struggling with what to do. In addition, having students reread directions when necessary, as well as to have students reword or restate the directions back to you, is another good strategy for comprehension, indicating they understand them.

5. The following chart shows the yearly average number of international tourists visiting Palm Beach for 1990–1994. How many more tourists that are international visited Palm Beach in 1994 than in 1991? *(Easy) (Skill 6.3)*

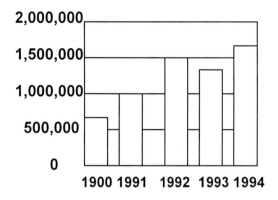

A. 100,000
B. 600,000
C. 1,600,000
D. 8,000,000

Answer: B. 600,000

The number of tourists in 1991 was 1,000,000 and the number in 1994 was 1,600,000. Subtract to get a difference of 600,000.

6. **Which statement is true about George's budget?** *(Easy) (Skill 6.3)*

A. George spends the greatest portion of his income on food.
B. George spends twice as much on utilities as he does on his mortgage.
C. George spends twice as much on utilities as he does on food.
D. George spends the same amount on food and utilities as he does on mortgage.

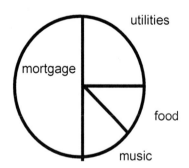

Answer: C. George spends twice as much on utilities as he does on food.

The graph shows that George spends twice as much on utilities as on food.

Read the following passage and answer the questions that follow.

Rainforests are an endangered habitat on our planet. Found primarily around the Equator, rainforests are categorized as climates with dense humidity, warm temperatures, and high amounts of rainfall—over 80 inches each year.

Extremely important to the Earth's ecology, rainforests provide homes to millions of plants, animals, and food resources. The plants of the rainforest generate rich oxygen for much of the Earth, and if their destruction persists, the damage to the rainforests will cause a dangerous threat to the planet's ecological balance. If the trees and plants fail to grow, the planet is deprived of many of the natural food resources of the rainforest, including cocoa, coffee, sugar cane, and many varieties of nuts, fruits and spices.

Rainforests also recycle air and clean water. The trees capture and remove a large amount of the carbon dioxide in the air. This decreases the temperature of the overall planet, therefore affecting the greenhouse effect, which traps heat in the Earth's atmosphere.

Land seizure is one of the leading threats to the rainforest. If this destruction continues, it will surely result in further critical environmental issues.

7. **Which statement best summarizes this passage?** *(Rigorous) (Skill 6.3)*

   A. Rainforests recycle water sources and provide many types of food resources as well.
   B. The Earth consists of many rainforests around its Equator, and they are an important habitat.
   C. Threats to the rainforest, including land seizure, are very dangerous to the rainforests' existence.
   D. Rainforests are currently an endangered habitat and the continued threats to them may be detrimental to the Earth's ecosystems.

Answer: D. Rainforests are currently an endangered habitat and the continued threats to them may be detrimental to the Earth's ecosystems.

Choice A provides more of a detail about the rainforest. Choices B and C begin to touch on a summary, but do not quite capture the best summary for the passage. Choice D includes that the rainforest is an endangered habitat that is important to the Earth's ecosystem.

8. **Which fact(s) from the passage would most likely <u>not</u> be included in a summary about this topic?**
    (Rigorous) (Skill 6.3)

    A. The rainforest traps the heat in the Earth's atmosphere.
    B. The rainforests are an endangered habitat.
    C. There are dangerous threats to the rainforest.
    D. The rainforests play an important role in the balance of the Earth's ecosystems.

Answer: A. The rainforest traps the heat in the Earth's atmosphere.

Choices B, C, and D all encompass the main idea of the passage—that the rainforests are endangered and the threats to them endanger the balance of ecosystems. Choice A is a detail about the rainforest.

Select the best answer for the following multiple-choice questions.

9. **Select the statement below that is true about journalistic writing.**
    (Average Rigor) (Skill 7.1)

    A. Journalism should contain biased statements.
    B. Journalism should convey information about a person, place, or event in a factual and objective manner.
    C. Using newspapers in the classroom is not a good tool for teaching.
    D. All of the above

Answer: B. Journalism should convey information about a person, place, or event in a factual and objective manner.

Journalistic writing should be free of bias, as it provides information about a person, place, or event using objective facts. Students should be routinely exposed to newspapers in the classroom, as they provide samples of "real-life" print sources.

10. **Which pairing below is the best example of matching an appropriate audience for the type of writing?** *(Average Rigor) (Skill 7.2)*

    A. Creative narrative story to a younger sibling
    B. Friendly letter with slang to a teacher
    C. History essay to a local politician
    D. Business letter to a friend

Answer: A. Creative narrative story to a younger sibling

Of these pairings, A is the best choice, as one might write a creative narrative to entertain a sibling. However, one is unlikely to write an informal friendly letter to a teacher, a history essay to a politician, or a business letter to a friend.

11. **When determining your tone and audience for a piece of writing, which of the following statements is likely to be the least considered?**
(Rigorous) (Skill 7.2)

    A.   What emotional qualities do I want to transmit in this writing?
    B.   What choice of language is best suited for my audience?
    C.   How lengthy should I make this piece?
    D.   What does the person already know about this topic?

Answer: C. How lengthy should I make this piece?

When determining the tone and audience for writing, answers A, B, and D are all important to consider. The length of the piece (C) is not as important as the other three elements.

Choose the underlined word or phrase that is unnecessary within the context of the passage.

12. **<u>Considered by many to be</u> one of the worst <u>terrorist</u> incidents <u>on American soil</u> was the bombing of the Oklahoma City Federal Building, which will be remembered <u>for years to come</u>.**
(Average Rigor) (Skill 8.1)

    A. Considered by many to be
    B. terrorist
    C. on American soil
    D. for years to come

Answer: A. Considered by many to be

Considered by many to be is a wordy phrase and unnecessary in the context of the sentence. All other words are necessary within the context of the sentence.

13. The <u>flu</u> epidemic struck <u>most of</u> the <u>respected</u> faculty and students of the Woolbright School, forcing the Boynton Beach school superintendent to close it down <u>for two weeks.</u>
(Average Rigor) (Skill 8.1)

   A. flu
   B. most of
   C. respected
   D. for two weeks

Answer: C. respected

The fact that the faculty might have been *respected* is not necessary to mention in the sentence. The other words and phrases are all necessary to complete the meaning of the sentence.

14. The <u>expanding</u> number of television channels has <u>prompted</u> cable operators to raise their prices, <u>even though</u> many consumers do not want to pay a higher <u>increased</u> amount for their service.
(Easy) (Skill 8.1)

   A. expanding
   B. prompted
   C. even though
   D. increased

Answer: D. increased

The word *increased* is redundant with higher and should be removed. All the other words are necessary within the context of the sentence.

Select the best answer for the following multiple-choice questions.

15. **Which of the following should not be included in the opening paragraph of an informative essay?**
(Average Rigor) (Skill 8.3)

   A. Thesis sentence
   B. Details and examples supporting the main idea
   C. A broad general introduction to the topic
   D. A style and tone that grabs the reader's attention

Answer: B. Details and examples supporting the main idea

The introductory paragraph should introduce the topic, capture the reader's interest, state the thesis, and prepare the reader for the main points in the essay. Details and examples, however, should be given in the second part of the essay, so as to help develop the thesis presented at the end of the introductory paragraph, following the inverted triangle method consisting of a broad general statement followed by some information, and then the thesis at the end of the paragraph.

16. **Which of the following should not be included in the opening paragraph of a creative writing piece?**
(Average Rigor) (Skill 8.3)

   A. Dialogue
   B. Thesis statement
   C. Introduction of characters and setting
   D. A style and tone that grabs the reader's attention

Answer: B. Thesis statement

The introductory paragraph of a creative writing piece would not have a thesis statement, as the thesis is used for expository writing.

For the underlined sentence(s), choose the option that expresses the meaning with the most fluency and the clearest logic within the context. If the underlined sentence should not be changed, choose Option A, which shows no change.

17.   Selecting members of a President's cabinet can often be an aggravating process. <u>Either there are too many or too few qualified candidates for a certain position, and then they have to be confirmed by the Senate, where there is the possibility of rejection.</u>
        (Rigorous) (Skill 9.2)

   A. Either there are too many or too few qualified candidate for a certain position, and then they have to be confirmed by the Senate, where there is the possibility of rejection.

   B. Qualified candidates for certain positions face the possibility of rejection, when they have to be confirmed by the Senate.

   C. The Senate has to confirm qualified candidates who face the possibility of rejection.

   D. Because the Senate has to confirm qualified candidates, they face the possibility of rejection.

Answer: C. The Senate has to confirm qualified candidates who face the possibility of rejection.

Option C is the most straightforward and concise sentence. Option A is too unwieldy with the wordy *Either...or* phrase at the beginning. Option B does not make clear the fact that candidates face rejection by the Senate. Option D illogically implies that candidates face rejection because they have to be confirmed by the Senate.

18.   Treating patients for drug and/or alcohol abuse is a sometimes difficult process. <u>Even though there are a number of different methods for helping the patient overcome a dependency, there is no way of knowing which is best in the long run.</u>
        (Rigorous) (Skill 9.2)

   A. Even though there are a number of different methods for helping the patient overcome a dependency, there is no way of knowing which is best in the long run.

   B. Even though different methods can help a patient overcome a dependency, there is no way to know which is best in the long run.

C. Even though there is no way to know which way is best in the long run, patients can overcome their dependencies when they are helped.

D. There is no way to know which method will help the patient overcome a dependency in the long run, even though there are many different ones.

Answer: B. Even though different methods can help a patient overcome a dependency, there is no way to know which is best in the long run.

Option B is concise and logical. Option A tends to ramble with the use of *there are* and the verbs *helping* and *knowing*. Option C is awkwardly worded and repetitive in the first part of the sentence, and vague in the second because it never indicates how the patients can be helped. Option D contains the unnecessary phrase *even though there are many different ones.*

19. **Many factors account for the decline in quality of public education. <u>Overcrowding, budget cutbacks, and societal deterioration, which have greatly affected student learning</u>.**
    (Rigorous) (Skill 9.2)

    A. Overcrowding, budget cutbacks, and societal deterioration, which have greatly affected student learning.

    B. Student learning has been greatly affected by overcrowding, budget cutbacks, and societal deterioration.

    C. Due to overcrowding, budget cutbacks, and societal deterioration, student learning has been greatly affected.

    D. Overcrowding, budget cutbacks, and societal deterioration have affected students learning greatly.

Answer: B. Student learning has been greatly affected by overcrowding, budget cutbacks, and societal deterioration.

Option B is concise and best explains the causes of the decline in student education. The unnecessary use of *which* in Option A makes the sentence feel incomplete. Option C has weak coordination between the reasons for the decline in public education and the fact that student learning has been affected. Option D incorrectly places the adverb *greatly* after learning, instead of before *affected.*

20. *Choose the sentence that logically and correctly expresses the comparison. (Easy) (Skill 9.2)*

    A. The Empire State Building in New York is taller than buildings in the city.

    B. The Empire State Building in New York is taller than any other building in the city.

    C. The Empire State Building in New York is tallest than other buildings in the city.

Answer: B. The Empire State Building in New York is taller than any other building in the city.

Because the Empire State Building is a building in New York City, the phrase *any other* must be included. Option A is incorrect because the Empire State Building is implicitly compared to itself since it is one of the buildings. Option C is incorrect because *tallest is* the incorrect form of the adjective.

In the sample paragraph below, chose the underlined transition that is not used effectively.

21. **Autumn is my favorite time of year. <u>First</u>, the crisp, clean air is refreshing after the humid days of summer. <u>In addition</u>, I love the cinnamon smells in the kitchen of apple pies and cider. I <u>also</u> enjoy the beautiful colors of the trees in autumn, too. <u>In contrast</u>, October brings my favorite holiday, Halloween, when everyone dresses up! <u>In sum</u>, the holidays, smells, and sights make autumn the best time of year.**
    (Average Rigor) (Skill 9.3)

    E. First
    F. In addition
    G. In contrast
    H. In sum

Answer: C. In contrast

In this paragraph, the transition *in contrast* is not used properly, as the statement that follows does not contrast with the other supporting sentences. Instead, a transition such as *finally*, would have been more suitable.

Select the best answer for the following multiple-choice questions.

22. **Transitional words and phrases help to**
    (Average Rigor) (Skill 9.3)

    A. Add structure to a text
    B. Signal relationships between ideas in a text
    C. Enhance the flow of writing
    D. All of the above

Answer: D. All of the above.

Transitions are words or phrases that signal relationships between ideas in a text. Proper use of transitional words and phrases add flow, fluency, and structure to a text.

23. **Which of the following is a complex sentence?**
    (Rigorous) (Skill 10.2)

    A. Anna and Margaret read fifty-four books during summer vacation.
    B. The youngest boy on the team had the best earned run average, which mystifies the coaching staff.
    C. Earl decided to attend Princeton; his twin brother Roy, who aced the ASVAB test, will be going to Annapolis.
    D. "Easy come, easy go," Marcia moaned.

Answer: B. The youngest boy on the team had the best earned run average, which mystifies the coaching staff.

Here, the relative pronoun *which* introduces a clause that comments on and is dependent on the independent clause, "The youngest boy on the team had the best run average."

Choose the most effective word within the context of the sentence.

24. **Many of the clubs in Boca Raton are noted for their _____ elegance.**
    (Average Rigor) (Skill 10.5)

    A. vulgar
    B. tasteful
    C. ordinary

Answer: B. tasteful

Tasteful means beautiful or charming, which would correspond to an elegant club. The words *vulgar* and *ordinary* have negative connotations.

25. **When a student is expelled from school, the parents are usually _____ in advance.**
(Average Rigor) (Skill 10.5)

A. rewarded
B. congratulated
C. notified

Answer: C. notified

Notified means informed or told, which fits into the logic of the sentence. The words *rewarded* and *congratulated* are positive actions, which do not make sense regarding someone being expelled from school.

26. **Before appearing in court, the witness was _____ the papers requiring her to show up.**
(Average Rigor) (Skill 10.5)

A. condemned
B. served
C. criticized

Answer: B. served

Served means given, which makes sense in the context of the sentence. *Condemned* and *criticized* do not make sense within the context of the sentence.

The passage below contains many errors. Read the passage. Then answer each test item by choosing the option that corrects an error in the underlined portion(s). No more than one underlined error will appear in each item. If no error exists, choose "No change is necessary."

Climbing to the top of Mount Everest is an adventure. One which everyone—whether physically fit or not—seems eager to try. The trail stretches for miles, the cold temperatures are usually frigid and brutal.

Climbers must endure severel barriers on the way, including other hikers, steep jagged rocks, and lots of snow. Plus, climbers often find the most grueling part of the trip is their climb back down, just when they are feeling greatly exhausted. Climbers who take precautions are likely to find the ascent less arduous than the unprepared. By donning heavy flannel shirts, gloves, and hats, climbers prevented hypothermia, as well as simple frostbite. A pair of rugged boots is also one of the necesities. If climbers are to avoid becoming dehydrated, there is beverages available for them to transport as well.

Once climbers are completely ready to begin their lengthy journey, they can comfortable enjoy the wonderful scenery. Wide rock formations dazzle the observers eyes with shades of gray and white, while the peak forms a triangle that seems to touch the sky. Each of the climbers are reminded of the splendor and magnifisence of Gods great Earth.

27. **Climbers must endure <u>severel</u> barriers <u>on the way, including</u> other <u>hikers</u>, steep jagged rocks, and lots of snow.**
     (Easy) (Skill 8.2)

     A. several
     B. on the way: including
     C. hikers'
     D. No change is necessary

Answer: A. several

The word *several* is misspelled in the text. Option B is incorrect because a comma, not a colon, is needed to set off the modifying phrase. Option C is incorrect because no apostrophe is needed after *hikers* since possession is not involved.

28. **A pair of rugged boots <u>is also one</u> of the <u>necesities</u>.**
    (Rigorous) (Skill 8.2)

    A. are
    B. also, one
    C. necessities
    D. No change is necessary

Answer: C. necesities

The word *necessities* is misspelled in the text. Option A is incorrect because the singular verb *is* must agree with the singular noun *pair* (a collective singular). Option B is incorrect because *if also* is set off with commas (potential correction), it should be set off on both sides.

29. **Plus, climbers often find the most grueling part of the trip is <u>their</u> climb back <u>down, just</u> when they <u>are</u> feeling greatly exhausted.**
    (Average Rigor) (Skill 10.1)

    A. his
    B. down; just
    C. were
    D. No change is necessary

Answer: D. No change is necessary
The present tense must be used consistently throughout; therefore, Option C is incorrect. Option A is incorrect because the singular pronoun *his* does not agree with the plural antecedent *climbers*. Option B is incorrect because a comma, not a semicolon, is needed to separate the dependent clause from the main clause.

30. **Climbing to the top of Mount Everest is an <u>adventure. One</u> which everyone—<u>whether</u> physically fit or not—<u>seems</u> eager to try.**
    (Rigorous) (Skill 10.2)

    A. adventure, one
    B. people, whether
    C. seem
    D. No change is necessary

Answer: A. adventure, one

A comma is needed between *adventure* and *one* to avoid creating a fragment of the second part. In Option B, a comma after *everyone* would not be appropriate when the dash is used on the other side of *not*. In Option C, the singular verb *seems* is needed to agree with the singular subject *everyone*.

31. <u>Climbers who</u> take precautions are likely to find the ascent <u>less difficult than</u> the unprepared.
(Average Rigor) (Skill 10.2)

A. Climbers, who
B. least difficult
C. then
D. No change is necessary

Answer: D. No change is necessary

No change is needed. Option A is incorrect because a comma would make the phrase *who take precautions* seem less restrictive or less essential to the sentence. Option B is incorrect because *less* is appropriate when two items—the prepared and the unprepared—are compared. Option C is incorrect because the comparative adverb *than*, not *then*, is needed.

32. If climbers are to avoid <u>becoming</u> dehydrated, there <u>is</u> beverages available for <u>them</u> to transport as well.
(Easy) (Skill 10.3)

A. becomming
B. are
C. him
D. No change is necessary

Answer: B. are

The plural verb *are* must be used with the plural subject *beverages*. Option A is incorrect because *becoming* has only one m. Option C is incorrect because the plural pronoun *them* is needed to agree with the referent *climbers*.

33. Each of the climbers <u>are</u> reminded of the splendor and <u>magnifisence</u> of <u>God's</u> great Earth.
(Rigorous) (Skill 10.3)

A. is
B. magnifisence
C. Gods
D. No change is necessary

Answer: A. is

The singular verb *is* agrees with the singular subject *each*. Option B is incorrect because *magnificence* is misspelled. Option C is incorrect because an apostrophe is needed to show possession.

34. By donning heavy flannel shirts, boots, and <u>hats, climbers</u> <u>prevented</u> hypothermia, as well as simple frostbite.
    (Average Rigor) (Skill 10.4)

    A. hats climbers
    B. can prevent
    C. hypothermia;
    D. No change is necessary

Answer: B. can prevent

The verb *prevented* is in the past tense and must be changed to the present *can prevent* to be consistent. Option A is incorrect because a comma is needed after a long introductory phrase. Option C is incorrect because the semicolon creates a fragment of the phrase *as well as simple frostbite*.

35. Once climbers are completely prepared for <u>their</u> lengthy <u>journey,</u> <u>they</u> can <u>comfortable</u> enjoy the wonderful scenery.
    (Easy) (Skill 11.3)

    A. they're
    B. journey; they
    C. comfortably
    D. No change is necessary

Answer: C. comfortably

The adverb form *comfortably* is needed to modify the verb phrase *can enjoy*. Option A is incorrect because the possessive plural pronoun is spelled *their*. Option B is incorrect because a semicolon would make the first half of the item seem like an independent clause when the subordinating conjunction *once* makes that clause dependent.

36. **Wide rock formations dazzle the <u>observers eyes</u> with shades of gray and <u>white, while</u> the peak <u>forms</u> a triangle that seems to touch the sky.**
(Rigorous) (Skill 11.3)

    A. observers' eyes
    B. white; while
    C. formed
    D. No change is necessary

Answer: A. observers' eyes

An apostrophe is needed to show the plural possessive form *observers' eyes*. Option B is incorrect because the semicolon would make the second half of the item seem like an independent clause when the subordinating conjunction *while* makes that clause dependent. Option C is incorrect because *formed* is in the wrong tense.

37. **The <u>trail</u> stretches for <u>miles,</u> the cold temperatures are <u>usually</u> frigid and brutal.**
(Rigorous) (Skill 11.4)

    A. trails
    B. miles;
    C. usual
    D. No change is necessary

Answer: B. miles;

A semicolon, not a comma, is needed to separate the first independent clause from the second independent clause. Option A is incorrect because the plural subject *trails* needs the singular verb stretch. Option C is incorrect because the adverb form *usually* is needed to modify the adjective *frigid*.

The passage below contains many errors. Read the passage. Then answer each test item by choosing the option that corrects an error in the underlined portion(s). No more than one underlined error will appear in each item. If no error exists, choose "No change is necessary."

Every job places different kinds of demands on their employees. For example, whereas such jobs as accounting and bookkeeping require mathematical ability; graphic design requires creative/artistic ability.

Doing good at one job does not usually guarantee success at another. However, one of the elements crucial to all jobs are especially notable: the chance to accomplish a goal.

The accomplishment of the employees varies according to the job. In many jobs the employees become accustom to the accomplishment provided by the work they do every day.

In medicine, for example, every doctor tests him self by treating badly injured or critically ill people. In the operating room, a team of Surgeons, is responsible for operating on many of these patients. In addition to the feeling of accomplishment that the workers achieve, some jobs also give a sense of identity to the employees'. Profesions like law, education, and sales offer huge financial and emotional rewards. Politicians are public servants: who work for the federal and state governments. President bush is basically employed by the American people to make laws and run the country.

Finally; the contributions that employees make to their companies and to the world cannot be taken for granted. Through their work, employees are performing a service for their employers and are contributing something to the world.

38.   **However,** one of the elements crucial to all jobs **are** especially **notable:** the accomplishment of a goal.
    (Average Rigor) (Skill 10.3)

    A. However
    B. is
    C. notable;
    D. No change is necessary

Answer: B. is

The singular verb *is* is needed to agree with the singular subject *one*. Option A is incorrect because a comma is needed to set off the transitional word *however*. Option C is incorrect because a colon, not a semicolon, is needed to set off an item.

39. The <u>accomplishment</u> of the <u>employees</u> <u>varies</u> according to the job.
    (Rigorous) (Skill 10.3)

    A. accomplishment,
    B. employee's
    C. vary
    D. No change is necessary

Answer: C. vary

The singular verb *vary* is needed to agree with the singular subject a*ccomplishment*. Option A is incorrect because a comma after *accomplishment* would suggest that the modifying phrase *of the employees* is additional instead of essential. Option B is incorrect because *employees* is not possessive.

40. In many jobs the employees <u>become</u> <u>accustom</u> to the accomplishment <u>provided</u> by the work they do every day.
    (Average Rigor) (Skill 11.1)

    A. became
    B. accustomed
    C. provides
    D. No change is necessary

Answer: B. accustomed

The past participle *accustomed* is needed with the verb *become*. Option A is incorrect because the verb tense does not need to change to the past *became*. Option C is incorrect because *provides* is the wrong tense.

41. Every job <u>places</u> different kinds of demands on <u>their</u> <u>employees</u>.
    (Rigorous) (Skill 11.2)

    A. place
    B. its
    C. employes
    D. No change is necessary

Answer: B. its

The singular possessive pronoun *its* must agree with its antecedent *job*, which is singular also. Option A is incorrect because *place* is a plural form and the subject, *job*, is singular. Option C is incorrect because the correct spelling of employees is given in the sentence.

42. In medicine, for example, every doctor <u>tests</u> <u>him self</u> by treating badly injured and critically ill people.
    (Average Rigor) (Skill 11.2)

    A. test
    B. himself
    C. critical
    D. No change is necessary

Answer: B. himself

The reflexive pronoun *himself* is needed. (Him self is nonstandard and never correct.) Option A is incorrect because the singular verb *test* is needed to agree with the singular subject *doctor*. Option C is incorrect because the adverb *critically* is needed to modify the verb *ill*.

43. Doing <u>good</u> at one job does not <u>usually</u> guarantee <u>success</u> at another.
    (Rigorous) (Skill 11.3)

    A. well
    B. usualy
    C. succeeding
    D. No change is necessary

Answer: A. well

The adverb *well* modifies the word *doing*. Option B is incorrect because *usually* is spelled correctly in the sentence. Option C is incorrect because *succeeding* is in the wrong tense.

44. In addition to the feeling of accomplishment that the workers <u>achieve</u>, some jobs also <u>give</u> a sense of self-identity to the <u>employees'</u>. *(Average Rigor) (Skill 11.3)*

    A. acheive
    B. gave
    C. employees
    D. No change is necessary

Answer: C. employees

Option C is correct because *employees* is not possessive. Option A is incorrect because *achieve* is spelled correctly in the sentence. Option B is incorrect because *gave* is the wrong tense.

45. **<u>For example,</u> <u>whereas</u> such jobs as accounting and bookkeeping require mathematical <u>ability;</u> graphic design requires creative/artistic ability.**
(Average Rigor) (Skill 11.4)

    A. For example
    B. whereas,
    C. ability,
    D. No change is necessary

Answer: C. ability,

An introductory dependent clause is set off with a comma, not a semicolon. Option A is incorrect because the transitional phrase *for example* should be set off with a comma. Option B is incorrect because the adverb *whereas* functions like *while* and does not take a comma after it.

46. **In the <u>operating room,</u> a team of <u>Surgeons, is</u> responsible for operating on many of <u>these</u> patients.**
(Easy) (Skill 11.4)

    A. operating room:
    B. surgeons is
    C. those
    D. No change is necessary

Answer: B. surgeons is

Surgeons is not a proper name so it does not need to be capitalized. A comma is not needed to break up *a team of surgeons* from the rest of the sentence. Option A is incorrect because a comma, not a colon, is needed to set off an item. Option C is incorrect because *those* is an incorrect pronoun.

47. **Profesions like law, <u>education,</u> and sales <u>offer</u> huge financial and emotional rewards.**
(Rigorous) (Skill 11.4)

   A. Professions
   B. education;
   C. offered
   D. No change is necessary

Answer: A. Professions

Option A is correct because *professions* is misspelled in the sentence. Option B is incorrect because a comma, not a semi-colon, is needed after *education*. In Option C, *offered*, is in the wrong tense.

48. **Politicians <u>are</u> public <u>servants: who</u> <u>work</u> for the federal and state governments.**
(Easy) (Skill 11.4)

   A. were
   B. servants who
   C. worked
   D. No change is necessary

Answer: B. servants who

A colon is not needed to set off the introduction of the sentence. In Option A, *were*, is the incorrect tense of the verb. In Option C, *worked*, is in the wrong tense.

49. **President <u>bush</u> is basically employed <u>by</u> the American people to <u>make</u> laws and run the country.**
(Easy) (Skill 11.4)

   A. Bush
   B. to
   C. made
   D. No change is necessary

Answer: A. Bush

Bush is a proper name and should be capitalized. Option B, *to*, does not fit with the verb *employed*. Option C uses the wrong form of the verb, *make*.

50. <u>Finally;</u> the contributions that employees make to <u>their</u> companies and to the world cannot be <u>taken</u> for granted.
(Average Rigor) (Skill 11.4)

A. Finally,
B. their
C. took
D. No change is necessary

Answer: A. Finally,

A comma is needed to separate *Finally* from the rest of the sentence. *Finally* is a preposition that usually heads a dependent sentence, hence, a comma is needed. Option B is incorrect because *their* is misspelled. Option C is incorrect because *took* is the wrong form of the verb.

XAMonline, INC. 21 Orient Ave. Melrose, MA 02176

Toll Free number 800-509-4128

TO ORDER Fax 781-662-9268 OR www.XAMonline.com

MASSACHUSETTS TEST FOR EDUCATOR LICENTURE - MTEL - 2008

PO#   Store/School:

Address 1:

Address 2 (Ship to other):

City, State Zip

Credit card number_____-_____-_____-_____   expiration_____

EMAIL _____

PHONE   **FAX**

ISBN	TITLE	Qty	Retail	Total
978-1-58197-287-0	MTEL Communication and Literacy Skills 01			
978-1-58197-876-6	MTEL General Curriculum (formerly Elementary) 03			
978-1-58197-607-8	MTEL History 06 (Social Science)			
978-1-58197-283-2	MTEL English 07			
978-1-58197-349-5	MTEL Mathematics 09			
978-1-58197-881-0	MTEL General Science 10			
978-1-58197-684-7	MTEL Physics 11			
978-1-58197-883-4	MTEL Chemistry 12			
978-1-58197-884-1	MTEL Biology 13			
978-1-58197-683-0	MTEL Earth Science 14			
978-1-58197-676-2	MTEL Early Childhood 02			
978-1-58197-893-3	MTEL Visual Art Sample Test 17			
978-1-58197-8988	MTEL Political Science/ Political Philosophy 48			
978-1-58197-886-5	MTEL Physical Education 22			
978-1-58197-887-2	MTEL French Sample Test 26			
978-1-58197-888-9	MTEL Spanish 28			
978-1-58197-889-6	MTEL Middle School Mathematics 47			
978-1-58197-890-2	MTEL Middle School Humanities 50			
978-1-58197-891-9	MTEL Middle School Mathematics-Science 51			
978-1-58197-266-5	MTEL Foundations of Reading 90 (requirement all El. Ed)			
			SUBTOTAL	
			Ship	$8.25
			TOTAL	

Saturday –
10:45
10:00
South...
24 Newton street

LaVergne, TN USA
09 November 2010
204171LV00001B/46/P